Making It Better

Making It Better

Activities for Children Living in a Stressful World

Barbara Oehlberg

Illustrated by Stéphanie Roth

 Redleaf Press

Published by Redleaf Press
a division of Resources for Child Caring
10 Yorkton Court
St. Paul, MN 55117
Visit us online at www.redleafpress.org

©1996 Barbara Oehlberg
Illustrated by Stéphanie Roth

Redleaf Press books are available at a special discount when purchased in bulk (1,000 or more copies) for special premiums and sales promotions. For details, contact the sales manager at 800-423-8309.

Library of Congress Cataloging-in-Publication Data

Oehlberg, Barbara, 1932-
    Making it better : activities for children in a stressful world /
Barbara Oehlberg ; illustrated by Stéphanie Roth.
      p.   cm.
    Includes bibliographical references and index.
    ISBN 1-884834-26-4
    1. Early childhood education—Activity programs. 2. Stress in children. 3. Stress management for children. 4. Grief in children. 5. School psychology.I. Title
LB1139-35.A37044   1996
372.146—dc20   96-41338
                                       CIP

Manufactured in the United States of America

Dedicated to Anneliese
who so poignantly demonstrated
to her grandmother how little
children are capable of
healing themselves

and to Nathan
who has been persistent
in teaching his grandmother
how to play.

Acknowledgments

James Garbarino, Ph.D., for the inspiration of his sustained dedication to children.

Bruce Perry, M.D., Ph.D., for the stunning advancements in understanding how violence affects young children.

Linda Catazaro, Kim Morgan, and Dawn Rucker for their support and typing.

The staffs of Captain A. Roth, Louis Pasteur, and Scranton Elementary schools in Cleveland, Ohio.

And my family, for enduring a messy dining room table for two years!

Table of Contents

Foreword

Teachers everywhere have sensed changes in children and their behaviors, particularly in the last several years. Children have not changed. Childhood has. The children around us are merely reflecting the challenging, sometimes scary changes in their environment and world.

What is a caring and exhausted teacher or caregiver to do? The amount of time left for learning activities after dealing with behavior problems seems to diminish weekly. Perhaps you have already come to the conclusion that many children are not learning as they might; more of the same is not going to help us achieve our goals for children.

I received very little preparation for how to respond to children who had never slept with a pillow they could call their own or eaten a warm meal at the same time several nights in a row. I was prepared to teach children who didn't have such issues and could leave lesser concerns at the doorstep as they came into school, ready to concentrate and learn. I suspect I was not alone.

Children living with uncertainty and insecurity have a difficult time focusing on learning. You may be the anchor needed to make sense out of that world. The opportunity to make a difference in children's lives has never been greater than it is today. You may be the best link between the children you care for and a viable future. For some children, you may provide the only opportunity for a responsive and supportive relationship through which the child can choose to invest in learning and commit to a future.

The world of childhood has changed and the opportunities for teachers have as well. Throughout this book you will find group activities that make it possible for children to engage in self-healing and self-empowerment. These activities enrich the learning process and help all children learn from their environments. Through this process they can integrate their life experiences into their learning experiences and begin to make sense out of a world that often seems threatening.

It is my sincere goal that through the activities in this book both you and the children you care for will find renewed trust, hope, and delight as together we embrace the twenty-first century.

Introduction: A Window of Opportunity

Why are America's children not learning as expected?

If the world in which children are growing up has changed, how can dedicated teachers and caregivers help children achieve their goals? Is it merely a matter of changing curriculum and setting high expectations?

This book is about bringing hope and confidence back to children and those who care for them. It attempts to translate the insights learned from medical research into activities that can help make a child's world look inviting and manageable again. It is about empowering children to understand the recent past and the present in order to reach for the future.

This book is about the healing and recovery necessary for children to be able to invest energy into their learning and development. It is about creating personal and educational successes.

The activities for healing and recovery are designed for classroom or small group use for children ages 3 - 10. They are intended to guide children into self-directed understanding and processing of experiences and memories. They are not intended to glean personal disclosures or to gather information about a child's experiences.

Experiences that can be traumatic for children are not always immediately recognized as a source of fear or loss by a caring adult. The key for a child is how the event was interpreted. For example, an adult knows that medical treatment serves an important purpose. To a young child, treatment can be bewildering and frightening. A parent sees moving to a new house as an exciting and satisfying achievement. To a child, it can be an overwhelming experience of separation, disconnectedness, and loss, which a child needs to grieve.

You will find children very capable of doing their own internal processing and healing. These silent "ah-ha's," followed by a deep exhaling, are personal and private and need to be respected as such. Group discussions would be advisable only when initiated by the children and comfortable for you.

There are three groups of activities: healing play, healing art, and healing language arts. They are designed to help children address their personal issues of loss, separation, rejection, despair, frustration, anger, and powerlessness.

Introducing these activities offers children the opportunity to understand situations and experiences that may have been confusing and beyond their control. This recovery process allows children to let go of those memories and move forward with their cognitive, social, and emotional development.

Choose activities based on the children's developmental skills. Children who have not mastered printing or writing skills may find the play and art activities most productive. These younger children can also benefit from the language arts with some adaptation on the adult's part, such as dictating words, using drawing instead of writing, and other creative ideas. Also, there is no cutoff age recommended for the activities since their purpose is to promote emotional healing and growth. An older child may need to backtrack to the developmental stage at which the traumatic experience occurred.

The healing play activities are a natural for preschool groups. Many of these activities can also provide an opportunity for elementary students to engage in positive, productive alternatives to acting-out behaviors before they become a habit. Healing language arts activities can even provide stress relief and empowerment for middle school students. Present the activities in the context of remembering how it felt to be a small child. Encourage the older children to think of what sort of story might be comforting to a young child.

Selection should be based on the developmental needs of the children, the group style, setting, and your interest or ease. No one is better suited to select the activities for the children you care for than you are; trust your intuition.

You will find none of the activities to be counterproductive or a waste of time for those children not specifically in need of healing. They all provide developmental or learning enhancements. This eliminates the need to identify, label, or separate those with a possible need for healing. The activities are neither a regimen nor a recipe for behavior management. They represent an opportunity for renewed hope and a sense of a future.

One caution to note—these activities are not intended to place teachers in a counselor's or therapist's role. Some children may need to be referred for assessment or individual counseling following the use of these activities.

The activities in this book are never to be used in place of mandated reporting of suspected child abuse or neglect.

Part

1

Childhood Changed

1 Trauma and Moving on to Hope

How Fears and Losses Affect Children

It is Monday morning, fifteen minutes into class, already Brian and James, two second graders in a city school, have been out of their seats three times, bickering and posturing, finally ending with a scuffle on the floor. Another week of classroom disarray in school. Another committed teacher frustrated and in dismay, aware that the performance test scores for this class are falling, not progressing. In a small town, halfway across the country, Jenny and Andre, two four year olds, are swearing and exchanging obscene gestures at their child care center. The staff shake their heads and wonder if there are any sweet, cute kids anywhere.

The statistics are repeated across the nation from urban centers to rural communities. Impulsive student aggressiveness is escalating while test scores are plummeting. Are these two realities interconnected? And more importantly, why is this happening now in your school, center, or home?

The reasons are multiple and complex. Children in America are growing up in a culture where violence is glamorized in entertainment and sports. It is not uncommon for children to witness violence within their homes or on the streets that surround them.

The reality is that children have witnessed frightening events, as a result of natural disasters or human activities, throughout history. Many recovered sufficiently and moved on to healthy development. What is different today is the combined effects of changes in the family and community, along with repeated exposure to real and fictional violent acts on the TV screens in their living rooms.

Young children are particularly vulnerable to the effects of violence. Children who witness family violence never feel safe. They experience persistent stress. Powerlessness and terror are prevailing feelings, even during "stable" periods.

But how does this connect with the acting-out behavior of Brian and James or Jenny and Andre on Monday morning?

Much brain cell growth and expansion takes place during early childhood. Growing up in a persistently threatening environment can interfere with the way a young child's brain develops. This can result in a greater concentration of brain cell growth in the midbrain at the expense of the cortex area, eventually limiting a child's ability to problem solve. It can also result in a predisposition to aggressive, impulsive behaviors and an underdeveloped capacity for empathy.

Children who demonstrate disrespectful and belligerent behaviors in school or other group settings are often doing so as a result of their arrested brain development, caused by their life experiences. They usually are not choosing to be disobedient, as such behaviors have been interpreted in the past. Struggling just to survive can limit children's brain development exclusively to the "flight or fight" instinct, greatly reducing their opportunities to solve problems.

As inappropriate as acting-out behaviors are, you can choose to interpret such aggressiveness as a child's pleading for an opportunity to feel safe, physically and emotionally. The angry, raging child may actually be a very frightened child. Traumatized children regularly demonstrate excessive vigilance and hyperactivity. These behaviors can sometimes be misinterpreted as Attention Deficit Disorder or Hyperactivity Disorder and the traumatic experiences of the child may be overlooked.

The brain research of Bruce Perry, M.D., Ph.D., of Baylor College of Medicine, referred to in this chapter, can help us learn why traumatized children find learning so difficult. Children who have been traumatized tend to be acutely perceptive of nonverbal clues. Their sensitive antennae decipher mood changes in a group before other adults or children, often accelerating their own internal turbulence.

Another important facet of trauma in children is that acting-out behaviors may not surface for six to eighteen months after the frightening event or loss. This can mean the child is in a different classroom with a different teacher who may know nothing about the house fire or family fatality that happened last year.

Children struggling with severe stress from trauma, also known as post-traumatic stress disorder, may experience flashbacks during the day and sleep disturbances at night. Flashbacks can be triggered by sounds, aromas, photos, and even seasonal changes. When these frightening and very real memories flood over children, they experience the terror all over again and the overwhelming feelings of helplessness return.

This research on brain development offers us opportunities for innovative breakthroughs. Activities that increase brain development will promote problem-solving abilities and decrease tendencies for aggressive behaviors. That is precisely what the activities in this book are designed to do.

Resources

Garbarino, J., N. Dubrow, K. Kostelny, and C. Pardo. *Children in Danger: Coping with the Consequences of Community Violence.* San Francisco: Jossey-Bass Publishers, 1992.

Herman, Judith Lewis. *Trauma and Recovery.* New York: Basic Books, 1992.

Osofsky, Joy, ed. *Children Youth and Violence: Searching for Solutions.* New York: The Guilford Press, 1995.

Peled, Einat, Peter G. Jaffe, and Jeffrey L. Edlesson. *Ending The Cycle of Violence: Community Responses to Children of Battered Children.* Thousand Oaks, CA: Sage Publications, 1995.

Perry, Bruce D. *Maltreated Children: Experience, Brain Development and the Next Generation.* New York: W. W. Norton, 1996.

• •

Breaking the Cycle of Violence

You might ask how anyone could suggest teachers take on another issue of society or be expected to perform yet another task. Those are reasonable concerns.

Healing activities seem to move the educational parameters beyond the initial expectations of everyone involved: teachers, administrators, counselors, unions, teacher colleges, caregivers, and even parents. Yet, many of us sense that doing more of the same is not getting us to where we and children need to be. In fact, we seem to be moving in the opposite direction.

You will find initiating healing activities adds very little to your personal duties. Adults often do not lead or manage the process or activity. The children themselves directly manage their own internal processing and recovery.

Traumatized children are frozen in a wordless vacuum, trapped in their terrifying memories and overwhelming sense of loss. When offered an opportunity to gently lift the cover from an encased terror, the angry energy seems to dissipate and the child finds some inner quiet.

Healing activities provide children with an opportunity to safely revisit frightening memories in a secure environment where they have access to a supportive, reassuring adult. The relief achieved can give stressed, fragile children the chance to trust and believe in a future, which is the essential foundation for healthy development and full learning capability.

For some children, fear has destroyed hope, which is itself terrorizing. Engaging in activities that permit children to address unresolved developmental issues can help them make some sense out of such frightening memories. Through their imaginations, children can change the way the people in their memory act and react, which can be empowering. By creating alternative outcomes through physical play or mental exercises in art and language, children can regain a sense of control over certain events and begin to believe in their future.

Children with unresolved developmental issues and terrors need opportunities to experience comfort and discover their own ability to comfort themselves. Our two-year-old granddaughter, Anneliese, clearly demonstrated that for our family.

Our daughter-in-law, Pam, called to ask about possible reasons for two-year-old Anneliese erupting into inconsolable sobbing whenever she pressed the button for one of the songs in her battery-operated musical book. This had happened three times, making her parents think about getting rid of the book.

When Pam said she had not sung that song to Anneliese since before they moved from their small, quiet apartment a year earlier, the pieces began to fit together. When Anneliese was thirteen months old, she and her family moved to a large house that they were remodeling. Anneliese's tranquillity was shattered by five days a week of carpenters sawing indoors.

There had been clues to Anneliese's bewilderment such as a faraway stare and a need to never let her mommy out of her sight. I failed to recognize these cues because of my need for denial. I preferred to think of her as being happy and joyful in her spacious new home. Nearly a year later, I was learning differently. Prompted by hearing the sounds of "You are My Sunshine" from her toy, Anneliese was grieving the loss of the stable secure world of her apartment—and she was doing it on her own.

I encouraged her parents not to get rid of the book and to affirm Anneliese's capacity to comfort herself through her tears whenever she listened to it. Several months later, Anneliese could hear the song without any tears. There also was a noticeable strengthening of her social skills.

For me this heartwarming and natural capability of a two year old to heal herself, nearly one year later, is convincing and renewing. However, I shudder when I remember how close we came to shutting down the healing process by almost throwing out the musical book all because the adults around her were uncomfortable with her sadness.

"Children are wonderfully receptive to experiencing the healing side of a traumatic reaction. Your job is simply to provide an opportunity for this to occur," said Peter Levine of the Ergos Institute in Colorado.

It is an exhilarating experience to stand back and watch children engaged in a healing activity work through beliefs of powerlessness and hopelessness. You can see in their faces, in the gaze of their eyes, that they are taking steps toward hope and resiliency.

Offering art projects, stories, or puppet plays can make connections with frightening memories and provide opportunities for children to work through unresolved trauma. Intuitive teachers know when children are struggling with events beyond their control. Trust your insights and provide the catalyst—an activity for healing. Current news events might provide a meaningful link between submerged memories and reality. Moving, medical care, or dealing with unfriendly dogs might be the key for some children and be topics of general interest for the rest of the children in the group.

Current events or national tragedies need to be addressed in open discussions. Your classroom or center may be the only safe place available for these children to confront their concerns, get rid of their anxieties, and hear reassurances. Reading the children's book *Why Did it Happen? Helping Children Cope in a Violent World*, by Janice Cohn (Morrow Junior Books, 1994) together could be a helpful activity for you and the children.

Traumatic experiences generate lots of energy within children. Until that energy is discharged, children cannot experience relief from their tension. Healing activities tend to tap into this energy. Reading or other routine activities can sometimes connect a child with a buried memory and generate a flashback or acting-out behavior. You may interpret this as an indicator of some success, not deliberate disobedience. Watch for these opportunities to introduce a healing activity.

It is natural for children to be agitated or cry while processing a loss or a traumatic memory. Your response to a child struggling with painful feelings will show the entire group of children how to provide care and support.

Some children may need gentle monitoring to assure their emotional security while engaged in the recovery exercise. There may be times when a child will need to leave the room to continue processing the experience and maintain personal dignity. This is advisable only when there is some other adult available for security and support.

The ultimate goal of the healing process is for traumatized children to realize they do not have to be helpless and powerless for the rest of their lives.

Healing activities are never to be used as a means of acquiring information from children or for diagnostic purposes. This should only be done by trained professionals.

 Resources

Banergee Associates. *Secret Wounds: Working With Child Observers of Family Violence.* Skillman, NJ, 1992, video.

Brohl, K. and P. Diaz. *Working With Traumatized Children: A Handbook For Healing.* Washington, DC: Child Welfare League of America, Inc., 1995.

Donovan, Denis M. and Deborah McIntyre. *Healing the Hurt Child.* New York: W. W. Norton and Co., 1990.

Johnson, Kenneth. *Trauma in the Lives of Children.* Almeda, CA: Hunter House, 1989.

Koplow, Lesley, ed. *Unsmiling Faces: How Preschoolers Can Heal.* New York: Teachers College Press, 1996.

Levine, Peter. "Understanding Childhood Trauma." *Mothering* 71 (1994): 48-54.

————. *Waking the Tiger: Healing Trauma Through the Body.* Longmont, CO: Ergos Institute, 1995.

Steele, William. *Kids on the Inside Looking Out After Loss.* Charlotte, NC: KIDS-RIGHTS, 1995.

Tobin, L. *What Do You Do With a Child Like This?* Duluth, MN: Whole Person Associates, 1991.

 Children's Books

Colm, Janice. *Why Did It Happen? Helping Children Cope in a Violent World.* New York: Morrow Junior Books, 1994.

Garbarino, James. *Let's Talk About Living in a World With Violence.* Chicago: Erickson Institute, 1993.

2 Childhood Losses: The Grieving Process

Supporting Grieving Children

All children experience losses as a necessary part of maturing. Many life-cycle losses, such as a lost pet, a best friend who moved away, or the death of a grandparent, are expected, experienced, and supported or affirmed by almost every human being. The impact of losses and separations that are not expected, such as a move into low-income housing after a divorce, a sibling's death from cancer, or brutal violence between family members, can overwhelm the coping skills of young children and their families or caregivers. This is especially true when one loss is coupled with another personal, family, or community challenge.

Sometimes the support systems and coping skills of the family and other adults in the child's life are inadequate to assist the child through the grief process. You can help significantly.

Losses, like other traumas children experience, are cumulative. Each new loss or separation can cause emotional pressure and reopen old wounds, contributing to a child's inability to believe in the future.

A sense of grief and loss is integral to the healing process. The grieving process is an essential component of recovery and is the focus of this book. Powerlessness, the sense of having no control over events, circumstances, or life itself, is the thread that unites grief and trauma. Anger serves as the glue that holds these strands together. When these strands are even lightly meshed, the ability to grieve is blocked.

The natural grieving process involves recalling images and memories of the deceased or inaccessible person or object. When dramatic horror and violence merge with the last image of that person, the child tends to shut out the overwhelmingly painful memory. Unfortunately, the grieving process shuts down before it can begin. In order for children to constructively grieve a violent loss, they must first process the trauma.

This chapter on grief, like this entire book, is focused on the deep-seated losses and traumas that show up in dramatic behavior changes months after the obvious event or tragedy.

Examining our own unresolved grief, feelings, and beliefs will help us support a grieving child. Adults who have not dealt with their own helplessness and sadness are unlikely to be able to help children who are struggling with grief and loss. When adults are unwilling or unable to respond to a child's grief, the child is forced to do it alone, which deepens the sense of loneliness. Many of us did not have the opportunity to observe adults interacting with grieving children, so we are uncomfortable when children cry about their loss. We want children to be happy.

Children who are grieving a loss simply want to be okay again. Our greatest gift to them is to believe in their return to wholeness even when they cannot. Children go through grief in stages similar to the way adults do. Like adults, children can slip in and out of stages, bouncing from one to another. As teachers and caregivers, we need to support children in this process so they can begin to understand the loss. Despite our caring, in the limited time we have with children, we may not be able to help them reach the acceptance stage of loss.

Preschool children usually see death as temporary and reversible. This view can interfere with their long-term healing because it is often compounded by anger and a sense of betrayal because the deceased person has not returned.

Adults may find it difficult to listen to children express anger toward the deceased. Your classroom, center, or home can become a haven for children to work through such feelings. Safety is the key to healing. Safe environments allow children to freely examine memories and feelings without any shame or rejection.

Young children tend to process grief in spurts or intermittently. It is easy for adults to misinterpret these interludes of relief as a sign that the child has completed the mourning process. Who has not heard an adult claim that since the child has forgotten the circumstances or topic, why bring it up and prompt sadness again?

You may find there are times when a grieving child cannot stay on task and would benefit from some private time. Providing some art supplies might help the child rebuild a sense of equilibrium. It is important to talk with the child about what will help create a more comfortable environment.

Despite outward clues of emotional calmness, children revisit their grief often. Holidays and anniversaries of the loss will be particularly stressful times for many years. Be on the alert.

The Stages for Processing Grief and Loss

1. **Denial and Shock—A state of disbelief**
   Seen as
   ◗ Flat emotions
   ◗ Compliant behavior
   ◗ Rhythmic movement for emotional release
   ◗ Clinging to mementos
   ◗ Prone to injury
   ◗ Development of real or imaginary illnesses

2. **Bargaining or Magical Undoing—An internal process of self-talk**
   Seen as
   ◗ Dramatic changes in compliance
   ◗ Perfectionism
   ◗ Dedication to something the child thinks will correct or change the reality of what happened

3. **Helplessness, Anger, Despair, and Depression—The physical and psychic expression of grief**
   Seen as
   ◗ Defiance and talking back
   ◗ Swearing
   ◗ Tantrums
   ◗ Fighting and hurting others, self, small animals, or property
   ◗ Regressing in development
   ◗ Withdrawal
   ◗ Guilt expressed through "if-only" comments

4. **Resolution and Understanding—A process of letting go of anger and guilt**
   Seen as
   ◗ Relaxed and at ease
   ◗ Improved concentration and focus
   ◗ Talking about the tragedy without becoming agitated

5. **Acceptance, Hope, and Resilience—The decision to go on living**
   Seen as
   ◗ Reflecting on the past and drawing strength from it
   ◗ Talking about the future
   ◗ Describing or seeing self in the future

One of the many challenges to grieving children is to allow themselves to express their feelings about the loss or separation. When a loss is sudden and unexpected, it intensifies the sense of helplessness in children. This perception of helplessness is caused more by the loss of control than the shock itself. You can help by offering encouragement, choices, and reassurances to grieving children. Let them know they are valuable, lovable, and important.

Grieving children need encouragement to continue dreaming. They need to grieve the dreams lost by their changed circumstance. Besides the loss of a person or situation, they have lost the vision of the way they thought life would be and how their needs would be cared for. Rather than trying to convince them everything is okay, honor their losses and need to grieve. We cannot talk them out of their grief. New dreams are the key to unlocking their hope.

Children, like adults, can be creative about hiding their fears and sense of powerlessness. Combative, acting-out behaviors are common defense mechanisms of grieving children, especially boys. Do not be fooled by their angry behavior.

If you are concerned that a child is deeply depressed, you need to refer the child for evaluation and counseling. See the appendix of this book for guidelines.

Just as children's expressions of mourning and powerlessness tend to be symbolic, healing strategies tend to be symbolic as well. Art, movement, and play become the symbolic language of grief resolution for children.

 Resources

Goldman, Linda. *Life & Loss: A Guide To Help Grieving Children.* Muncie, IN: Accelerated Development, Inc., 1994.

Lagorio, Jeanne. *Life Cycle: Classroom Activities for Helping Children Live with Daily Change and Loss.* Tucson, AZ: Zephyr Press, 1993.

• •

Issues and Experiences that Compound Loss, Separation, and Grief

Incomplete Attachments: Reactive Attachment Disorder (RAD)

Infants who receive adequate nurturing—are fed, held, and rocked when they cry—have optimal brain development. Babies that are not provided this type of care experience arrested development in the area of the brain that takes in and interprets information. This failure in the attachment process during the first two years of life contributes to reactive attachment disorder (RAD).

Children with RAD are difficult to reach and exhibit behavior that can be hard to understand. The world becomes a very challenging place for them. Children with RAD sense they are not having the same experiences other children their age are having. They are also highly vulnerable to loss in their lives and display an inordinate need to be in control.

Trust in people is difficult for children and youth with RAD and can be a sign that a child has RAD. Other ways to tell if a child has RAD include temper tantrums and bullying; body rigidity; motor skill difficulties; and fascination with pain, gore, and fire.

 Resources

The Attachment Center at Evergreen
    P.O. Box 2764
    Evergreen, CO 80439
    (303) 674-1910
    Newsletter: $5.00 per year.

Karen, Robert. *Becoming Attached: Unfolding the Mystery of the Infant-Mother Bond and Its Impact on Later Life.* New York: Warner Books, 1994.

Magid, Ken and Carole A. McKelvey. *High Risk: Children Without A Conscience.* New York: Bantam Books, 1987.

Changes in Status: New Sibling

Young children can be dramatically affected by a new baby in their home. This is true whether the addition is through birth, adoption, or foster care. To a preschooler, this change can be overwhelming and disorienting, particularly if it follows some other loss experience such as a move, change in caregiver, or change in health status.

Preschoolers can become terrified that their parents no longer love them. Most children are aware that families replace things when they no longer serve their purpose or are wanted. This idea can prompt children to interpret the new baby as a message they are no longer wanted or loved. They feel powerless, rejected, and angry. Behavioral changes may not show up for several months. Trust your intuition and offer some healing activities that will allow the child to get rid of any fears or jealousy.

Children can communicate these feelings and anxieties through behaviors such as nightmares, which cause them to be tired in school; nail biting; hair pulling; muscle aches; stuttering; irritability; teasing; excessive shyness, possessiveness, or generosity; meekness; and "grazing" play in which they wander from toy to toy, unable to engage in real play.

Children's Books

Boyd, Lizi. *Sam is My Half Brother*. New York: Puffin, 1990.

Delton, Judy. *Angel's Mother's Baby*. Boston: Houghton Mifflin, 1989.

Stein, Sara Bonnett. *That New Baby: An Open Family Book for Parents and Children Together*. New York: Walker & Co., 1994.

Changes in Home or Residence

Home is the cornerstone of a child's world. Moving, even when it is to a bigger or more deluxe building, involves a separation and loss that children need to mourn.

Home to a child is filled with memories, which are woven together with its unique aromas and sounds. These sensory imprints, even those experienced before children can speak, allow them to relax, settle back, and breathe deeply at home.

Even in homes where emotional and physical safety are not routine, most children claim a room, area, or corner as their space—the place where they feel freer to do their dreaming. The loss of these familiar and predictable senses have to be mourned before children can embrace their new dwelling place and rebuild their perceptions of security.

It is only natural that these changes will show up in children's behavior in school. By providing predictable, consistent routines and guidelines you will be reinforcing the sense of security and stability for the child who has recently moved. This helps them use their emotional energy to cope and learn.

Seasonal and religious holidays may bring back feelings and memories of a child's previous home. This may preoccupy a child or interfere with the child's ability to participate in activities.

Children's Books

Blume, Judy. *Are You There God? It's Me Margaret*. New York: Dell Publishing, 1986.

McKend, Heather. *Moving Gives Me A Stomachache*. Buffalo, NY: Firefly Books, Ltd., 1988.

Changes in School or Center Environments

There are many reasons why a change in school or caregiver may be necessary. Regardless of the cause, frequent changes can be stressful for a child.

A natural reaction of children stressed by frequent moves is to avoid investing energy in new friendships or relationships. Some of that resistance may be directed toward you, their new teacher. Children who frequently move are grieving past losses and attempting to avert the pain and disappointment of again having to say good-bye and separate.

The challenges to a child's sense of security and social development include negotiating the new streets and neighborhood routes, neighborhood codes of status and turf for children, school or center social codes and regulations, and teacher style and expectations.

All of these challenges are in addition to the family changes and the circumstances that prompted the move. Like children jealous of a new child in their home, these children can communicate their feelings and anxieties through behaviors such as nightmares, which cause them to be tired; nail biting; hair pulling; muscle aches; stuttering; irritability; teasing; excessive shyness, possessiveness, or generosity; meekness; and "grazing" play in which they wander from toy to toy unable to engage in real play. You might also see disruptive outbursts, tattling, excessive vigilance, and nearly complete withdrawal.

Resources

Smith, Charles A. *The Peaceful Classroom: 162 Easy Activities To Teach Preschoolers Compassion and Cooperation.* Beltsville, MD: Gryphon House, 1993.

Children's Books

Brillhart, Julie. *Anna's Goodbye Apron.* Morton Grove, IL: Albert Whitman & Co., 1990.

Osborne, Judy. *My Teacher Said Goodbye Today.* Brookline, MA: Emijo Press, 1987.

Shles, Larry. *Do I Have To Go To School Today?* Rolling Hills Estates, CA: Jalmar Press, 1989.

Changes in Health or Wellness of Child or Family Member

Changes in children's health and the medical care they receive can be terrifying. Suddenly their world has changed in addition to the physical effect of the accident or disease itself. The very foundation of security has been altered for them as the predictability of what they know as normal or routine has changed. The result of such experiences may not surface as behavior changes until months later.

In spite of repeated, caring explanations by family and medical staff, it is difficult for young children to understand why the intrusive medical treatment, which to children can feel assault-like, was necessary.

After being able to return to the school or caregiver, such children may still be struggling with their perception of themselves in their world. This may include a sense of insecurity and memories of powerlessness. As a receptive teacher or caregiver you might choose to introduce some healing activities that would address those dilemmas.

Changes in the health of a family member can generate similar feelings and behaviors in children. Like other losses, children may grieve the change in family life caused by new physical limitations on a parent such as no longer being able to play outside together. They also may be afraid by the bewildering array of equipment such as tubes or needles seeming to invade their loved one.

Feelings of powerlessness and fear are natural in these circumstances and are often compounded by guilt. Young children sometimes assume they have caused the illness or accident of a parent or sibling by having been angry at that family member. Sometimes children may actually get sick in the hope that the illness or injury will be transferred to them. Children with such burdens need to have their feelings and conditions respected. A referral for counseling might be considered.

The attention focused on the sick family member can generate ambivalent feelings for the children in the family. Added to the mix of fear and stress may be jealousy. These feelings may surface as behavior changes because the child trusts you and sees the environment shared with you as an emotionally safe place.

Frequent communication with the child's family can provide insight and understanding. By sharing puzzling comments or behaviors, both you and the family will be better at translating and clarifying any misinterpretations by the child.

 Children's Books

Havill, Juanita. *The Magic Fort.* Boston: Houghton Mifflin Co., 1991.

Merrifield, Margaret. *Come Sit By Me.* Ontario, Canada: Women's Press, 1990.

Nelson, Vacinda. *Always Grandma.* New York: South China Printing Co., 1988.

Parkinson, Carolyn. *My Mommy Has Cancer.* Rochester, NY: Park Press, 1991.

Stein, Sara Bonnett. *A Hospital Story: An Open Family Book.* New York: Walker and Co., 1984.

Changes in Family Makeup and Support

The death or unavailability of a family member, caregiver, or sibling can create a shattering loss for children. Since young children formulate their self-identity through the reflections of themselves by prime caregivers, the loss of one of those caregivers represents a partial loss of self. The death of a sibling brings the realization that a similar fate is a possibility for any child.

The divorce or separation of parents can be debilitating to a child. Memories of bickering, fighting, or perhaps violence leading up to the divorce may compound the feelings of loss and separation and lead to a sense of betrayal. Both of the adults are the child's parents and loyalty to both becomes confusing if not impossible. The mourning process for a child following a divorce may not be compatible with the needs of the custodial parent.

Once again, your setting may be the only environment in which children can work out these feelings and rebuild a sense of control over their lives.

Other family changes can also affect children's sense of stability and their ability to achieve. A parent's reentry into the paid work-force can require profound changes and transitions for children. The loss of employment by a parent or caregiver or the addition of a relative to the household also may have destabilizing effects in the classroom or center.

Any activity that addresses powerlessness, loss, or anger can help mourning children heal themselves.

Children's Books

Berman, Claire. *What Am I Doing in a Step-Family?* New York: Lyle Stuart, 1982.

Clifton, Lucille. *Everett Anderson's 1,2,3.* New York: Henry Holt and Company, 1992.

Cochran, Viei. *My Daddy Is A Stranger.* Omaha: Centering Corporation, 1992.

Hickman, Martha. *When Andy's Father Went To Prison.* Niles, IL: Albert Whitman & Company, 1990.

Quintan, Patricia. *My Daddy Takes Care of Me.* Ontario, Canada: Annick Press, 1987.

Sanford, Doris. *Please Come Home.* Portland, OR: Multnomah Press, 1985.

Loss of Sense of Security

There is hardly a child in America who has not learned the world can be dangerous and hostile. Words and images of violence pervade their recreation, entertainment, neighborhoods, and for some, their homes.

Today's children sense the adults around them cannot guarantee the safety of any child. This seemingly universal awareness is reinforced for many children by their parents' similar conclusions. Parents and teachers may not even be aware of children's feelings of insecurity and fear. The adults themselves often have not faced the reality of how the world has changed for children. Such denial of the changes in our world can lead to an inability or unwillingness to understand children's acting-out behavior as a need for security. Despite adult denials, countless children have no sense of a future. The window of opportunity to change that perception in children is brief.

How can teachers and parents make children aware of potential harm or disaster without increasing their sense of insecurity? Every time a child hears cautions such as, "Don't go there because it's too dangerous!" their sense of security is decreased.

Children need to mourn this generalized loss of security, or needed sense of safety that they have never had. Some need to address this from an even more personal and tragic perspective.

Children who live in violent households have a dramatic need to process and cope with the unavailability of their family and the lack of nurturing they need.

These situations raise complications for teachers and children involving loyalties, respect for parents, and the social norm that claims what happens behind closed doors is an individual family's business.

Family violence, such as spousal abuse or child abuse, can destroy children's innate capacity for empathy and compassion and replace it with anger, cynicism, and a need for revenge. A child living in a violent family can never establish a sense of security as long as the abuser is a member of the household. Children know they cannot stop an adult or older sibling from abusing, so they live in fear and powerlessness every hour of every day.

There are many fragile children in our nation's schools and child care centers. As the teacher of a child who has witnessed violence or experienced insecurity, you have a challenging opportunity to provide an environment that guarantees emotional and physical safety. You may be the main support for such a child to trust their sense of self and their feelings. Through the gift of your acceptance and support, the child can be empowered, healed, and learn to trust. Such efforts are paramount to stopping the cycles of violence and passive helplessness.

Children's Books

Berry, Joy. *About Traumatic Experiences.* Chicago: Children's Press, 1990.

Colm, Janice. *Why Did It Happen? Helping Children Cope in a Violent World.* New York: Morrow Junior Books, 1994.

Davis, Diane. *Something Is Wrong In My House.* Seattle: Parenting Press, 1984.

Gabarino, James. *Let's Talk About Living in a World With Violence.* Chicago: Erickson Institute, 1993.

Williams, Vera. *A Chair for My Mother.* New York: Morrow, 1992.

Loss of Self-Worth

Self-worth depends on a child's opportunities to demonstrate competence, mastery, and industry. When such opportunities are blocked for some reason, children are intuitively aware of the lost opportunities and their growing sense of powerlessness. Trusting in their ability to shape their future is essential for children's mental health. Children whose experiences do not include opportunities to develop a sense of control will need to process their anger about perceived unfairness. Such losses of self-worth can be helped by healing activities that address anger, powerlessness, and loss.

Whenever children are shamed, at home, school, or in the neighborhood, they anguish over this personal loss of dignity and integrity. Repeated experiences of shame can destroy children's resiliency and capacity to believe in themselves or their future unless healing and empowering opportunities are available.

All forms of child abuse generate deep shame and loss of self-esteem and innocence. Ridicule and verbal attacks can be almost as devastating as physical or sexual abuse. Physical discipline such as spanking is equally undermining to children's sense of self-worth.

Most states have eliminated corporal punishment in public institutions. Many children, however, experience spanking and other physical discipline outside of school. It may not be a teacher or a center's role to intervene in a family practice of spanking, but giving children the opportunity to work through the feelings generated by such experiences can help them from feeling helpless or acting violent as an adolescent and adult.

Resources

Curwin, Richard L. and Allen Mendler. *Am I In Trouble? Using Discipline To Teach Young Children Responsibility.* Santa Cruz, CA: ETR Associates, 1990.

Johnson, Dorothy Davis. *I Can't Sit Still. Educating and Affirming Inattentive and Hyperactive Children.* Santa Cruz, CA: ETR Associates, 1992.

Levin, Diane E. *Teaching Young Children In Violent Times: A Preschool-Grade 3 Violence Prevention and Conflict Resolution Guide.* Cambridge, MA: Educators for Social Responsibility, 1994.

Tobin, L. *What Do You Do With A Child Like This: Inside the Lives of Troubled Children.* Duluth, MN: Pfeifer-Hamilton Publishers, 1991.

Children's Books

Blackburn, Lynn. *The Class in Room 414.* Omaha: Centering Corporation, 1987.

Clifton, Lucille. *Everett Anderson's Goodbye.* New York: Henry Holt and Company, 1992.

Maple, Marilyn. *On The Wings of A Butterfly.* Seattle: Parenting Press, 1992.

Mellonie, Bryan and Robert Ingpen. *Lifetimes.* New York: Bantam, 1983.

Sanford, Doris. *Don't Look At Me.* Portland, OR: Multnomah Press, 1986.

———. *It Must Hurt A Lot.* Portland, OR: Multnomah Press, 1986.

Simon, Normal. *I'm Not A Cry Baby.* New York: Puffin Books, 1989.

Temes, Roberta. *The Empty Place.* Far Hills, NJ: Small Horizons, 1992.

Thomas, Jane. *Saying Goodbye to Grandma.* New York: Clarion Books, 1988.

Tiffault, Benette. *A Quilt for Elizabeth.* Omaha: Centering Corporation, 1992.

3 Healing from Trauma and Loss

Healing through Play

Every child has the potential for developing self-confidence and positive self-esteem. However, some children have had experiences that have closed down their access to that potential.

Confusing or frightening experiences that traumatize young children rob them of their personal power, creating a sense of powerlessness. Choices and options seem to be nonexistent. There is just silent shame.

Healing play can help with this. Healing play is play through which children project their internal world onto toys or through role playing. Children displace their feelings, wishes, or trauma and symbolically play out their experience in an attempt to understand and make sense out of the memory.

A goal of healing play is to nudge children into problem solving and strengthen their abilities to make good choices. This healing is empowering and integral to reinstating hope.

For hurting children to develop and trust their ability to solve problems and shape their futures, you must believe they can. Believing in their potential may be your greatest gift to the children you care for.

Young children may lack the language skills that would allow them to tell adults how they see their world and themselves. Preschool children, especially hurting ones, often cannot use words to define or describe their feelings or needs. For young children, spontaneous play becomes the most natural vehicle for self-expression.

Healing play provides an additional dimension for hurting children by offering an opportunity for them to process a traumatic experience. Through healing play, children can begin to discharge feelings and develop new understandings of the experience and their memories of it. Through symbolic play, children can transform the helplessness they have experienced into personal powerfulness. Healing play certainly will not change the outcome or reality of the original frightening event, such as injury or death, but it can provide the child with a developmentally meaningful way to process, accept, or tolerate the memory.

By making your space a safe environment for expressing feelings through words and activities, you can give the children the opportunity to work through their defenses and memories. To take such emotional risks and start the recovery process, however, fragile children must have freedom from rejection, ridicule, or shame.

Transformation takes place when children actively confront the memories locked within themselves. Issues or topics that are never talked about can remain submerged and corrosive for years. Healing play activities provide a symbolic way to address these unresolved issues and make it possible for children to process the memory and redirect their impulsive energies more constructively.

To bring up frightening experiences and reopen wounds seems uncaring and harsh to many adults even when it is done symbolically. It can be awkward at first, especially if we have unresolved issues of our own.

You will find, however, children yearn to put confusing issues to rest. They want to understand and let go of the bothersome memories. Just as they can heal the scrapes on their knees, in most cases, they can heal their psyches.

Children who have witnessed brutal violence may need to repeat or reenact with toys that aggressive act. Acting out a brutal scenario using toys on toys is often a clue that a child has witnessed a disturbing event. Fantasy aggression is not real aggression. Difficult as it may be for adults to observe this form of play, it is essential for healing to take place and needs to be allowed. Telling the child such play is inappropriate will certainly shut down the recovery.

Adult supervision is essential to assure physical and emotional safety for everyone in the room. You may need to define boundaries without shutting down the symbolic play process. For example, say, "All of us in this room need to be safe and have our own feelings."

Traumatized children often compulsively repeat a specific play pattern that is related to their confusing or frightening experience. Children can remain stuck in a repetitive play pattern for months, even years, never finding relief or moving toward a resolution. Your role is to guide the child toward a reworking of the experience being played out in order to modify or change the outcome.

Traumatized children, locked into compulsive play patterns, can benefit from having a calm, caring adult ask open-ended questions that nudge the child toward an alternative resolution of the situation they are reenacting. Problem-solving questions, like the ones listed below, will help the child move toward a healthier play outcome. Through healing play, children can transform the helplessness they experienced into a proactive, symbolic powerfulness.

Such questioning also encourages the children to use the part of their brains which may be undeveloped beyond the fight or flight instinct.

Children do not need to orally respond to these questions. Their answers will be seen by changes in their behaviors as their stress is reduced.

Questions to Facilitate Healing Play

What happens next?

I wonder what Teddy hopes will happen next?

I wonder what Teddy wishes would happen differently?

I wonder what Teddy means by that?

I wonder what it means to be (mad, sad, scared)?

I wonder what Teddy wishes would change?

And then what?

Tell me, could it have been worse?

I wonder if the doll likes to feel that way?

What is the doll going to say now?

And then how will the doll feel?

I wonder what the toy could do differently?

What does the toy want to say?

What's the best thing that could happen?

How does the toy want to feel?

I wonder why the toy would do that? What do you think?

Is Teddy afraid something will happen?

What is it that Teddy doesn't like?

Why do you think Teddy does that?

Can you tell me, is Teddy scared or mad?

Well, it's okay for Teddy to be angry. What might Teddy be able to do about it?

Healing play always remains child directed. You do not lead, criticize, or interpret it. You are the catalyst for such play and can facilitate its direction toward an alternative outcome for the child.

However, some emotionally fragile children may not be able to play because they are preoccupied with survival issues and the violence that swirls around them. They may first require from you assurances that they are safe and worthy of being comforted. They may need a trusting relationship with a particular adult and a transitional object or toy.

There may be opportunities for you to privately and gently assist children in altering their misunderstanding or distortions regarding the frightening memory. Try not to talk children out of their beliefs, rather, move them toward a greater understanding of the event and its memory through problem-solving questions.

If at all possible, consult with the child's parents or guardian about your insights. They may have vital information and be better positioned to clarify perceptions. This was poignantly exemplified to me during a training program. In our third session, Joanne, one of the teachers, excitedly shared an experience prompted by our last session, which included a discussion of ritualistic play and sharing information with parents.

Joanne and her co-workers had been concerned for Mae, a four-year-old girl, whose father had died the previous spring. Mae appeared more reserved and passive since returning that fall than she had during the months immediately following her father's death. Mae had developed a pattern of unusual daily play that confused Joanne. Although it presented no classroom disturbance, this observant teacher had not been able to understand why every day Mae would unscrew the lid of a toy baby bottle, fill the bottle with sand, replace the lid, and place the bottle on a nearby shelf.

After our session on ritualistic play and using parents as a resource, Joanne consulted Mae's mother and learned that Mae's father had been cremated and the ashes were placed in a small jar. Through collaboration, Mae's mother and Joanne helped Mae understand the memorial practice and why it had been carried out. The daily play pattern soon ended and Mae, once fragile, could go on with developmental growth.

Although healing play is child-directed, there are specific ways adults can support and facilitate the play toward constructive resolutions for young children. Again, the goal is not to elicit direct verbal responses from children but to enhance the processing of their memories or perceptions and support children in moving forward toward empowerment.

As tempting as it may be, you cannot suggest any changes in the actual outcome of the original tragedy. The event, regrettable or sad as it may be, is completed and over. It is important that you are supporting young children as they learn to deal with the reality of their world.

Making your area or room a place that supports children's healing brings another challenge to a caring adult. In order to provide the "tools" for the symbolic replay of traumatic memories, play areas should include toys, props, and settings that match a child's real living environment.

Environments that support healing play may need to reflect negative but realistic settings that match children's daily experiences and surroundings. For example, in a front porch setting, a bench or rocking chair probably should not be freshly painted. A worn stuffed sofa or a section of cyclone or picket fence in ill-repair may also be realistic.

Witnessing violence within families is recognized as the first lesson in aggression and powerlessness for many children. Plastic or cloth sets of family figures or dolls, representing the diversity of the community, can become props for replaying family dynamics. Animal family sets serve equally well. Tongue depressor puppets, which depict family members or family roles, are inexpensive and appealing to young children. Tongue depressor puppets of community service people can complement family characters for more complex play. Firefighters, police officers, emergency teams, doctors, and nurses would be some examples.

Issues of power, dominance, and powerlessness are central to many frightening memories of children. Toys that depict various power levels and sizes can provide opportunities to work through these dilemmas. Friendly dinosaurs, dragons, monsters, elephants, and lions are favorites of all children because they combine great size with the capacity to protect and care. At the opposite end of the scale, insects and baby animals are enticing tools for working through size and power issues with preschoolers.

Toy telephones can provide a young child a safe way to talk through events or experiences and create outcomes more to the child's choosing. Imaginary conversations can become an effective way to discharge energized feelings through words without directly harming anyone.

The professional goals of caring teachers are to promote social skill advancement and academic or cognitive growth. Unfortunately, children whose development has been arrested by a traumatic experience cannot engage in age-appropriate development or cognitive achievements until they have successfully understood and integrated their terrorizing memories.

Providing toys that match what children encounter in their lives can become an important prop for reenacting the events that have generated traumatic memories. This creates a dilemma about allowing toy guns to be used. Are aggressive behaviors being encouraged or are healing opportunities being nurtured? Even play therapists do not agree on this issue.

Children bringing toy guns, knives, and other instruments of violence to the classroom creates dilemmas for preschools. For a school or teacher to provide such toys is usually inconceivable. But not all young children have healthy environments and constructive experiences. The decision to provide toy versions of instruments of violence for symbolic healing play requires frank and extensive discussion by all staff members. The final decision needs to be one of personal choice based on a full understanding of all the risks and consequences.

 Resources

Gil, Eleana. *The Healing Power of Play: Working With Abused Children.* New York: Guilford Press, 1991.

Koplow, Lesley, ed. *Unsmiling Faces: How Preschools Can Heal.* New York: Teachers College Press, 1996.

Lagorio, Jeanne. *Life Cycle: Classroom Activities for Helping Children Live with Daily Change and Loss.* Tucson, AZ: Zephyr Press, 1993.

Schaefer, Charles and Kevin O'Connor, eds. *Handbook of Play Therapy.* New York: John Wiley & Sons, 1983.

Singer, Dorothy G. *Playing for Their Lives: Helping Troubled Children Through Play Therapy.* New York: The Free Press, 1993.

Webb, Nancy B., ed. *Play Therapy with Children in Crisis: A Casebook for Practitioners.* New York: The Guilford Press, 1991.

Part
2
. . . . .

Activities for Empowerment

4 Healing Play

Guided Play

Each activity in this book lists what issues it is designed to address, the purpose of the activity, the materials needed, and how to do the activity. The issues might be readily observable in some children and not apparent at all in others; however, the activities will be helpful for most children in today's complex world. The activities do not recommend ages but instead rely on your judgment. In general, most activities are appropriate for ages three to ten; however, a child's developmental stage is often a better guide to whether an activity is appropriate and developmental stages do not always correspond with expected ages.

Select the healing activities that you sense will best match the needs, skills, and interests of the children you care for, regardless of age or grade. No one in your school or center knows and understands these children better than you do. Trust your experience and intuition.

Play is a learning tool for children everywhere and is appropriate for elementary and preschool classrooms. Consider the needs and interests of the children you care for and choose the hands-on learning activity that best matches those needs, particularly their emotional and developmental needs.

The subjects or topics of some play or hands-on activities could easily become the format or outline for a creative writing activity for older children who prefer literary exercises. Feel free to make adaptations that will best suit the children you care for.

Tell the Telephone

Issues

Emotional insecurity, separation, a need to be cared for.

Purpose

To provide an opportunity for children to anonymously and safely express their needs and hopes.

Materials

Unconnected real or realistic toy telephones.

Procedure

Encourage children to tell the telephone their needs and wishes whenever they want to. Explain that it is important for them to express their secret desires. Be sure to explain that although their wishes and hopes are important to state, expressing them will not change what has happened. Explain to them that adults and children often feel better after talking about their needs or worries.

The Wish Box

Procedure

Encourage the children to draw a picture of a wish or hope that is important to them and place it in the Wish Box. Explain that if they take special care to look at the inside of the lid they will see a special person who will always be with them, while they think about ways to make the wish work out.

Issues

Emotional insecurity, separation, a need to be cared for and valued.

Purpose

To provide an opportunity for children to express needs and hopes and recognize the one person (themselves) always available to them for meeting their needs.

Materials

Brightly decorated box with a hinged lid, covered by a mirror on the inside, paper, and crayons.

Hide and Find

Procedure

Encourage the children, one by one, to hide a stuffed animal somewhere in the room. Have the same child look for it and celebrate finding it. Model for them the caring language and gestures they might use. Affirm each child's personal celebration.

Issues

Separation, loss, emotional insecurity.

Purpose

To create opportunities for children to experience the joy of reuniting.

Materials

Favorite stuffed animal.

Magical Glasses

Issues

Distrust of environments and adults.

Purpose

To provide opportunities to build security and trust.

Materials

Children's plastic sunglasses and several pieces of different colored cellophane.

Procedure

Give the children colored cellophane and encourage them to look through the different colors. Discuss how items in the room, such as classmates, look different through different colors but stay the same without the colored cellophane. Introduce and explain that the statement "looking at the world through rose-colored glasses" means everything looks bright and hopeful. Consider these questions for discussion: How might someone use their imagination to change the way a place looked and how they felt about it? Looking through what colors might make a place look safe? Comforting? Peaceful? Relaxing?

Encourage the children to wear their sunglasses if they need or want to change their view of the room so it is more comfortable for them.

Suggestions

Read the children *Ship of Dreams* by Dean Morrissey (Abrams, 1994).

ACTIVITY 5

Caring for "Boo-Boos"

Issues

Emotional insecurity, a need to be comforted.

Purpose

To provide opportunities for children to discover their capacity to care for others and help themselves at the same time.

Materials

Washable doll, red washable paint, a small paint brush, paper towels or small sponges, and bandages.

Procedure

Using a washable doll, explain to children that the doll has been hurt. With a small paint brush, place a little red paint on the doll's knee or arm. Coach the children to use caring words for the doll. Demonstrate how to clean the wound and place a bandage on the area.

Variations

Use yourself as an example and ask a child to volunteer to help you clean your wound and apply a bandage.

Ask children to find a partner and take turns being the caregiver and wounded party. Dab a little red paint on the area they select for their wound. Provide cleaning materials and bandages for caregivers. Reverse roles.

Suggestions

Discuss the feelings and importance of being and having caregivers. What did it feel like when you heard the words of comfort and caring? How did it feel when you said the words of comfort to a friend or classmate? Would you enjoy saying those kind words more often?

ACTIVITY 6

Rescue Teams

Issues

Physical insecurity, emotional insecurity, a need to be cared for.

Purpose

To provide an opportunity for children to develop courage and learn to cooperate with and care about others.

Materials

Stuffed baby animals, sheet or blanket, and wide ribbon or rope.

Procedure

Tell the children a story about a little kitten who gets lost. For example, a little kitten gets lost under a thick cluster of bushes. A group of children walking home from school hears the kitten's scared and lonely sounding meows. The children decide to form a rescue team by linking their hands one to another and carefully inching the first child under the bushes to rescue the kitten. The first child passes the kitten down the rescue chain, to the next child. From hand to hand, each child comforts the kitten with words and strokes. Have the children discuss their feelings about the story.

After the story, drape the sheet or blanket over a low table and place the stuffed animal under the table. Guide groups of about four or five children in becoming a rescue team for the toy animal.

Variations

Tell the same story as in the first procedure, then assist children in forming rescue teams to come to the aid of a "lost" or separated child. Create a divide by placing a ribbon or rope on the floor. Have the rescue team lead their classmate to safety amid greetings of joy and caring. Repeat as needed.

Suggestions

Ask the children who could become a rescue team for them if they ever need one at home or in their neighborhood.

ACTIVITY 7

Care-Wrapping

Issues

Emotional insecurity, a need to be comforted or cared for.

Purpose

To provide opportunities for children to discover their capacity to care for others and help themselves at the same time.

Materials

Large stuffed toy or doll and stretchable bandages (such as ACE bandages) cut into two-foot lengths.

Procedure

Explain to the children how a toy or doll has fallen and injured its arm or leg and hurts. Using comforting words, carefully and gently apply the bandage, securing it with masking tape.

Variations

Using yourself as an example, ask a child to volunteer to bandage your arm.

Ask children to form teams of three, and taking turns, have one child pretend to be injured and the other two act as caregivers.

Mother Hens

Issues

Physical insecurity, emotional insecurity, a need to be protected.

Purpose

To provide an opportunity for children to protect others and help themselves at the same time.

Materials

Large fans or woven trays.

Procedure

Tell the children a story about a mother hen whose little chicks have no feathers to protect themselves from the rain. During the story, use fans or trays as simulated wings and show how the mother hen would use them to protect her chicks. As you repeat the story's details, add sound effects of the mother hen clucking. Have the children make the sounds of the chicks peeping as they seek shelter and protection.

Ask the children to form teams of five or six and give each team two fans or trays. Designate who will play mother hen and have them perform the story. Repeat, allowing each child to have a turn as mother hen providing safety and protection by holding up or spreading out the fans as make-believe wings.

Suggestions

Discuss the children's feelings about the story. What did it feel like when you were being protected? What were your feelings when you were being the mother and protecting others?

ACTIVITY

9

Big and Little Lions

Issues

Vulnerability, a need to trust.

Purpose

To provide an opportunity for children to experience and practice being gentle and powerful.

Materials

Paper or cardboard crowns and music.

Procedure

Discuss that lions are often called the king of beasts and what that means—powerful, courageous, and fierce. Then talk about lions being parents with little lion cubs to care for and protect. Explain that they have to be tender and gentle at the same time they are powerful and fierce. Wearing a crown to pretend you are a lion, demonstrate gentleness by giving a gentle hug to each child. Be sure to ask each child if you can hug them.

Since this game involves hugging, ask the children who wants to play as a lion (a hugging role) and, for those uncomfortable giving or receiving hugs, who wants to play as a jungle tree (a watching role). Of the lion children, give crowns to half the children who will be lion kings, and ask the other half to be lion cubs. With music playing, have the children walk in a circle growling or meowing according to their role. When the music stops, the lion kings have to find a cub and gently hug them. Discuss gentleness beforehand.

Suggestions

Play the first round as described. For each additional round give out more crowns, adding to the number of lion kings, creating bigger and bigger hugging bunches, until finally everyone participating will be a lion king, hugging each other gently.

ACTIVITY
10

Magic Wands of Courage

Issues

Fear, a need to feel courageous.

Purpose

To build courage by allowing children to appreciate and respect their fears while learning they can confront them.

Materials

Plastic drinking straws, large gold stickers, strands of curling ribbon, a stapler, and a variety of stuffed animals.

Procedure

Demonstrate how to make wands by stapling a large gold star and several strands of curling ribbon to one end of a straw.

Tell the children a story about two lost bunnies. For example, there were two little bunnies who were having such a good time playing, that they paid no attention to where they were hopping. Suddenly, they heard a noise they did not recognize and were very frightened. They looked around and realized they did not recognize one single tree or bush and did not know which way to hop to get home. They were lost.

They became so fearful, they were frozen and could not move. Just then, a squirrel climbed down from a tree above them, and waved a Magic Wand of Courage in front of them (demonstrate). The squirrel asked them questions to help them.

The squirrel asked, "Did you hop past the fence that's over there?" (point toward an imaginary fence). "Did you hop past the gentle swooshing fir tree that's over there?" (point in another direction). "Did you hop past the apple tree that's over there?" (point in yet another direction). The bunnies, who were now completely unfrozen, thought over the questions and remembered passing the apple tree. They joyfully hopped in that direction, past the tree. Discuss how using our thinking powers can help us find solutions and feel confident. Ask the children if the wand brought the solutions or if the questioning and thinking did.

Help the children to make their wands.

As a group, consider similar situations of fear of being lost for toy animals that have been selected and placed around the room. Have the children use their Magic Wand to help each animal build the courage needed to stay safe. Have them ask the toy animal questions such as these: How could you feel safer? How could you find your way back to safety?

Suggestions

Encourage the children to use imaginary Magic Wands of Courage to help themselves use their thinking powers and their courage in situations such as losing sight of a parent in a store, hearing surprising noises or not remembering where the house key is.

ACTIVITY 11

Hands of Courage

Procedure

Talk about issues of danger and safety with the children, including the importance of thinking through ways to stay safe and being courageous.

Show pictures of situations or objects that could be dangerous to the children and discuss why they may be dangerous. Have the children figure out how they can help a younger child who is moving toward something dangerous. Ask them what words they could use so the other child would not panic.

Pass out gloves and mittens, telling the children they now each possess symbolic "Hands of Courage." Discuss how they can imagine wearing the gloves during times when they need protection.

Have children explain how they might use their imaginary "Hands of Courage" to rescue a young child in one of the situations they have just discussed, and how they would bring the child to safety. Repeat as necessary, using different pictures.

Issues

Physical insecurity, a need for safety and protection.

Purpose

To provide an opportunity for children to protect others and help themselves at the same time.

Materials

Pictures of situations or objects that could be dangerous to young children, such as the water's edge, ladders, campfires, or lawnmowers. A collection of gloves and mittens.

ACTIVITY 12

Meeting Nightmares

Issues

Fear caused by night-mares or flashbacks.

Purpose

To help children regain power and control over their fears.

Materials

The children's book *Sandy's Suitcase* by Elsy Edwards (SRA, Macmillan/McGraw Hill, 1994), paper, pencils or crayons, tape, and a suitcase or briefcase (optional).

Procedure

Read *Sandy's Suitcase* to the children. Encourage them to name items they would find helpful in their suitcase if they were packing one as Sandy did for meeting her nightmares. Hand out paper and pencils and have the children draw the items they would want to bring. Children then can fold the paper in half and tape it shut to represent an imaginary suitcase. If a real suitcase is available, have each child stick his or her paper in the suitcase.

Walking Bravely

Procedure

Tell the following story.

One day a little girl named Annie was walking her puppy, Edgar, who was sniffing and exploring every bush and tree along the sidewalks. Annie did not notice that Edgar was lagging farther and farther behind her.

Edgar came to a fenced-in yard and was just beginning to sniff at the fence when suddenly a great big dog ran up to the fence from the inside of the yard and barked very fiercely. Edgar was terrified!

Annie turned around to see where Edgar was when she heard the big dog barking, and she was frightened too. Edgar had nervously stopped walking, and was whining and yelping. Annie was too afraid to walk back to rescue her puppy.

Issues

Physical insecurity, emotional insecurity, a need for safety and protection.

Purpose

To help children start to overcome their fears.

Materials

A wide ribbon or rope and a stuffed, toy puppy.

Ask the children what Annie could do. Encourage suggestions that would keep Annie, Edgar, and the barking dog safe. Offer the suggestion that maybe Annie could sing a song to encourage herself, then sing this song to the children.

"If you're scared and you know it, stop and think.

"If you're scared and you know it, stop and think.

"If you're scared and you know it, it's okay, you can control it.

"If you're scared and you know it, stop and think."

Finish the story by telling the children that when Annie heard herself say the words of the song, she was able to find her courage and walk past the barking dog behind the fence and rescue her puppy.

After telling the story, teach children to sing the song. Ask for volunteers to be Annie, Edgar, and the big barking dog. Place a ribbon or rope on the floor to represent the fence. Have every child play the role of the child. Repeat as needed.

Bells of Courage

Issues

Physical insecurity, emotional insecurity, a need for protection and safety.

Purpose

To help children start to overcome their fears.

Materials

A bell (with a handle if possible).

Procedure

Tell the following story:

Long, long ago, in a land far away, there was a happy village of people. The people in the village loved their children and knew that their children's greatest joy was eating fresh blueberries. Now blueberries grow wild in the forest, so someone had to go deep into the woods to pick them.

Each summer, the village asked which teenagers would volunteer to pick the blueberries and each summer a few offered to go into the woods, but none of them ever came back. So one summer, one of the mothers decided to silently follow the teenagers, being careful never to let them see her.

When far, far into the woods, the teenagers found big, delicious berries, which they picked as they wandered deeper and deeper into the woods. They did not watch where they were going, or how they had gotten there.

When it started to get dark, they realized they were lost and allowed their fear to freeze them into statues. When the mother saw this, she rang the bell she always carried with her, which surprised the teenagers and woke them from their fear. They used their courage and their strength of mind to follow the sound of the bell and find their way out of the woods.

Ask the children what a rescue team does and when a rescue team would be needed.

Talk about places or situations that can be scary for children. Have the children act out the situations and take turns ringing the bell to wake each other from their fears. Help them build their courage by having them act out or talk about their return to safety. Ask them how a child who overcame a fear might feel. Ask how a child can keep a feeling of courage from day to day.

ACTIVITY 15

Releasing Worries

Issues

Powerlessness.

Purpose

To get children to recognize that they can let go of issues they have no control over.

Materials

Balloons, small pieces of paper, and pencils.

Procedure

Encourage the children or an individual child to write worries, fears, or secrets on a small piece of paper. Place the paper into a balloon, blow it up, tie the balloon, then release it into the air. Let the children watch it float away, and imagine their worries going with it. Discuss with the children how this makes them feel.

Variations

To avoid releasing balloons into the environment, give each child an envelope or small paper bag in which to insert their note. Close or seal them and then place them into a larger bag or box. Ask the children to help decide where to send or deliver the collection.

5 Healing Art

Guided Art

Art activities can provide children with meaningful opportunities to process hurtful, traumatic experiences and losses. Healing art activities offer children the chance to put feelings into forms or shapes and release memories and sensations. By guiding art activities for children, we help them use art to symbolically express preverbal experiences similar to the way healing play does.

Drawing can be a comfortable tool or technique because it allows children to communicate symbolically and get rid of unhappy feelings about incomprehensible experiences and frightening memories. Direct inquiry seldom leads to productive understandings for children. We are all familiar with a child's response of "I don't know!", or a shrug of the shoulders to our questions of "Why?" or "What made you do that?"

Drawing provides children with a safe, nonthreatening opportunity to connect with memories that are confusing or scary. Through the drawing or other art form, a child can symbolically work out an alternative or resolution that brings relief from the frightening memory. Regardless of their level of language development, traumatized children can relieve themselves from their perceptions of powerlessness and helplessness through drawing.

Children can find healing art a safe way to express experiences and memories without identifying or labeling persons or events. Healing art activities are empowering for children because they can control the event and behavior of others to create a desirable outcome. They can freely connect with their dreams and hopes through expressive art, knowing they alone hold the key to the real meaning of the piece. It becomes a safe, risk-free way to express their needs and desires.

Healing art activities can give children another way to understand their feelings and learn that feeling bad does not mean that they are bad.

Finally, healing art activities give teachers and other caregivers insights into how children see their world and themselves in that world. Although these insights are not for diagnosis, they will increase your understanding of each child. Some children may need referral for assessment and individual help. If you suspect this, please see the guidelines for referral in the appendix.

Wearing a Heart on My Sleeve

Issues
Unexpressed feelings.

Purpose
To help children identify, respect, and communicate feelings.

Materials
Variety of colored paper hearts (laminated hearts are an option) and double-stick tape or regular masking tape.

Procedure

Post colored hearts on a wall along with a list of suggested meanings for the colors. You may use the list here or encourage children to select their own meanings for the colors.

Blue = Sad

Blue-Green = Worried

Brown = Frustrated

Dark Green = Comforted

Gold = Strong

Green = Cooperative

Navy Blue = Scared

Orange = Angry

Pink = Jolly or silly

Purple = Betrayed

Red = Happy

Silver–Blue = Lonely, brittle, cold inside

Yellow = Hopeful

Encourage the children to wear hearts, when they want, to communicate how they are feeling. You and other adults should also participate. These hearts could be reusable and stored in a special place.

Drawings for Power

Issues

Powerlessness.

Purpose

To help children feel, in a positive way, more powerful and in control.

Materials

Paper, crayons, pencils, paint, and brushes.

Procedure

Have the children or individual child draw a picture of the following people, places, and situations:

Someone the child can always talk to.

A place where the child can always feel safe.

A scary dream or experience. (After drawing it, have the child tear it up and destroy it.)

The same or another scary dream, but adding someone or something that allows the child to feel safer.

Someone the child trusts and respects.

Someone who trusts the child.

A monster who looks angry, sad, lonely, scared, or happy.

A house or place where the child can feel protected and safe.

A house or place where the child might not feel safe or protected. (After drawing it, have the child change the house or place so that it could be safe.)

A home where the child once lived and would like to see again.

A school or classroom that would be a welcoming, friendly place in which to be.

Something the child would like to take from the classroom when the child moves on to a new room or school. (After drawing it, if it is an ugly or unpleasant picture, have the child change it so that it is more comfortable or pleasing to the child.)

Something that could be called or titled "anger," "sad," or "scary."

A wish or hope of how the child wants to feel today.

A mad, scary face. (After drawing it, have the child change it to be less scary.)

A dog the child would like to have as a companion. (Please note, if a child is frightened, he will often draw large fierce dogs. If a child is lonely, she will often draw a small lap dog.)

A monster protecting a treasure. Have the child show how to get past the monster to get to the treasure.

An animal the child would choose to be for a day.

Discuss the drawings with the children, asking them to tell you only what they want to about the pictures. Accept what they say and affirm their right to have and express their feelings.

ACTIVITY 18

The Teardrops of My Heart

Issues

Loneliness, insecurity, fear of rejection.

Purpose

To help children learn to express their inner feelings.

Materials

Precut blue teardrops, at least three by six inches big, double-stick tape or regular masking tape, and pencils or pens. (The teardrops can be laminated on one side if desired.)

Procedure

Encourage everyone in the room, including adults, to wear a teardrop over their heart, as needed, for comforting and healing. If they want, they can describe their sadness—in a drawing or written in code—on the back of the teardrop where it faces their heart.

Wishing Rainbow

Issues

Hopelessness, powerlessness.

Purpose

To connect children with their dreams and wishes and translate them into possible actions.

Materials

Colored paper cut into two and one-half inch by eight inch strips, double-stick tape or masking tape, markers or crayons, scissors, and a large poster board securely hung on the wall.

Procedure

Discuss rainbows and what they mean to people. For example, ask if the children think rainbows mean good or bad luck. Ask if they know any songs about rainbows, such as "Somewhere over the Rainbow."

Offer the children strips of colored paper and ask them to write or draw their dream or hope for comfort and happiness. When they have finished this, arrange the strips in an arch across the upper portion of the poster board in the form of a rainbow.

Next, ask the children to draw around their hand on colored paper. Have the children cut out the shape or use precut hands of colored paper. Encourage the children to think of important wishes or dreams and decide what they might do, starting today, to make that wish or dream come true or begin to come true. They can draw or write their wish or dream on the hand.

Place their action hand under the rainbow. Allow this to be a long-term, ongoing project as needed.

Color Out All of the Anger and Sadness

Procedure

Suggest that children, when they need to, take a red-orange crayon and color out all of the anger within them. Ask if they can feel the anger moving through their arms and hands as it leaves their body and becomes the color on the page.

Suggest that children, when they need to, take a blue crayon and do the same to color out all of the sadness or loneliness within them.

Ask the children what they can do, if they want to, to change their feelings. Ask what color they would color themselves when they choose to get angry when another person is angry. Then ask them what color they would color themselves when they choose not to get angry when another person is angry.

Issues

Powerlessness, anger, loneliness, sadness.

Purpose

To teach children they have the ability to change their feelings and to comfort themselves.

Materials

Crayons and unlined paper.

Coloring Solutions

Issues

Poor problem-solving skills, powerlessness.

Purpose

To increase children's problem-solving skills and self-esteem.

Materials

Unlined paper and crayons.

Procedure

Ask the child or children to choose and color how they feel when they do not know how to solve a problem or change a situation. Encourage them to think about what it feels like to be blocked and decide what color would best describe that feeling. Let them color or draw whatever they choose in that color. Then have them pick a color that describes how they feel when they know what they might do in a difficult situation.

Ask the children what they can do for themselves so they can change the way they are feeling. Have them pick a color that represents the new feeling and write or draw in that color.

Ask the children to color the way they might feel inside when they are hearing words or information they did not want to hear. Then ask them to think about how those feelings can be erased or changed with a new color representing a more comforting feeling. Let them color with the new chosen color.

ACTIVITY 22

Caring Coupons

Procedure

Discuss and explain coupons. What are they used for? By whom? When? Are they free or does a person have to buy them?

Explain that coupons do not have to be used only at a store and that they can make coupons for "Gifts of Caring" to be used when they want a hug or a smile. Hand out 3"x 5" cards and ask the children to decorate one side and on the other side write the Gift of Caring they choose. For younger children, you can write the suggestions for Gifts of Caring for them. Encourage them to give the coupons to others at home or school when they want to receive or give a little caring.

If you have two different colors of cards, use one color for *giving* care coupons, and another color for *receiving* care coupons.

Examples of Gifts of Caring to give to others:

I will play with you today.

I will smile at you today.

I will be your special friend today.

I will give you a hug today.

I will sit next to you today.

I will comfort you today.

Examples of Gifts of Caring to ask to receive from others:

I need a smile today.

I need a hug today.

I need your friendship today.

I need your comfort today.

Issues

Feeling unloved and unlovable.

Purpose

To help children discover their capacity to care for others and help themselves at the same time.

Materials

Pencils, crayons, and unlined 3"x 5" cards in two different colors, if possible.

Portraits of Loving Memorials

Issues

Grief, loss, separation from a loved one.

Purpose

To help children learn to comfort themselves.

Materials

Crayons, paint or pencils, and unlined paper or photocopies of picture frames you draw yourself.

Procedure

Ask the children to visualize the look of someone or something they long for and miss. Discuss how losing something or someone important can be sad and how people often worry they might lose the memory. Ask them how someone could be certain to never forget that valued person, toy, or pet. Have the children draw a picture of the treasured memory on the unlined paper or on the paper with the frame photocopied on it. Encourage the children to consider the safest place they could keep their treasured memory. Discuss how they might be able to recall that memory without actually looking at it or having it in front of them. Would they have to look at the picture to remember?

ACTIVITY 24

Portraits of Trust and Friendship

Issues

A sense of being disconnected.

Purpose

To help children identify and strengthen bonds or attachments.

Materials

Crayons, paint or pencils, and unlined paper or photocopies of the picture frames that you draw yourself.

Procedure

Have the children draw a picture of someone who trusts them, and of someone they trust. When the picture is finished, encourage them to write what they would like to say to or hear said by the person in the picture. Younger children can tell you the words and you can write them.

ACTIVITY 25

Safety Badge

Procedure

Ask the children to think about what they could carry with them to make them feel safe and secure. Give them guidelines on what items would also ensure that others around them are able to feel safe.

After the discussion, give the children precut, colored badges. Ask them to draw or write on their badge the item or idea that makes them feel safe. Offer replacements until they are satisfied with their drawing. For protection and durability, laminate the badges or place them in plastic sandwich bags and tape shut. Tape the safety pin to the badge and pin on the child or, if pins are not available, attach with masking tape.

Allow the children to wear their badges whenever they feel the need to.

Issues
Insecurity.

Purpose
To help children develop a sense of security.

Materials
Crayons or pencils; precut, colored badges you draw yourself; laminating materials or clear sandwich bags; and safety pins or masking tape.

ACTIVITY 26

Safety Shields

Procedure

Talk about what a shield is and what kind of shield the children would need to feel safe at all times. For example, what might such a shield be made of and what would it look like?

After the discussion, help the children decide the shape of their shield. Use the brown paper or newsprint sheets to make a pattern in the desired shape. Trace or transfer the shape to cardboard and cut it out. Have the children decorate the shield in a way that represents what it would take to make them feel safe. With the strapping tape, attach the fabric strip to the back side of the cardboard to create a handle.

Discuss with the children how they can pretend to carry and use their imaginary shield, even when it is not with them.

Issues
Insecurity.

Purpose
To help children develop a sense of security.

Materials
Medium cardboard in a variety of colors about two feet by three feet, markers or crayons, strapping tape, sturdy fabric such as denim cut into one inch by twelve inch strips, and brown paper or sheets of newsprint.

The Healing Garden

Issues

Hurt, anxiety, insecurity.

Purpose

To encourage children to comfort and heal themselves using their imagination.

Materials

Crayons, markers, paint, and paper.

Procedure

Talk about the beauty of gardens and how their buds might be thought of as hope and their blossoms as joy. Look at pictures of gardens. Explain that most of us are not able to be in such beautiful gardens every day, but we can create our own garden in our imagination and go there whenever we want.

After the discussion, pass out art materials and have the children draw their idea of a healing garden or a place they could visit in their imaginations whenever they need to comfort themselves.

Suggestions

Encourage the children to think about who they would like to invite to visit them in their healing garden.

ACTIVITY
28

Dream Family

Procedure

Explain what a foster or adoptive family is. Then tell a story of a child, Henry, from a land far away who traveled to a new city because his parents had died in an accident. Henry had been told he would live with the Cassidy family on Oak Street. But when he got to the house on Oak Street, no one named Cassidy lived there. So, the grown-ups in the city offered Henry the chance to choose the family of his dreams. Although Henry never forgot his first family, he found ways to be happy with his new family.

After the story, ask the children to consider what they would have selected if they had been Henry. Have them draw a picture of that dream family. Assure the children the meaning of their picture will remain personal and private to them.

Issues

Lack of empowerment or sense of control.

Purpose

To help children affirm their right to make choices and have dreams.

Materials

Crayons or paint and paper.

Love Bank

Issues

Emotional insecurity, feeling unloved.

Purpose

To help children discover their capacity to care for themselves and others.

Materials

A plastic canister with a lid, a lock, and red or pink paper hearts about five or six inches big.

Procedure

Briefly explain the banking system and concept of making deposits in order to have money available for withdrawals when needed. Then talk about other types of banks, such as blood banks and food banks.

After the discussion, tell the children they are going to set up a love bank. Explain that the canister will be the bank for their love. Encourage the children to write thoughts of joy or love on the hearts and deposit them in the canister bank. Younger children can draw joyful pictures or color with loving and joyful colors. Explain that the hearts will stay in the bank for a day when someone may need to make a withdrawal.

Establish a procedure that from now on everyone can make a deposit when they have extra good memories and feelings, and they can make withdrawals on days when they need comfort and care for themselves or to give to a friend or classmate.

Caring Quilts

Issues

Physical and emotional insecurity, fear or memories of being lost, loneliness.

Purpose

To recognize children's worries, provide support, and teach them to identify their options.

Materials

Paper or cloth squares, fabric or regular markers, and glue and a large sheet of paper (quilt size), or a sewing machine.

Procedure

Ask the children if they have heard of quilts that are called comforters or security blankets. Ask if anyone knows what those terms could mean, why someone would want one with either name and what benefits they might have. Explain that the class is going to make one of these together and let them decide whether to call it a comforter or security blanket.

Provide each child with a square of cloth or material and markers. Ask them to decorate their square with the design that represents safety, security, or comfort to them. When each child's square is completed, attach them with glue on a larger sheet of paper or sew together.

Suggestions

Read *The Boy Who Spoke Colors* by David Gifaldi (Houghton Mifflin Co., 1993).

Power Hats

Issues

Powerlessness, insecurity, fear, confusion.

Purpose

To encourage children to trust in their problem-solving skills and internal power.

Materials

Unlined paper or photocopies of familiar occupational hats, that you draw yourself.

Procedure

Discuss how certain hats worn by people tell us who the wearer might be or what type of work they do. Talk about the personal characteristics that are often associated with the wearers of some hats: firefighters in their hats are considered brave, nurses in their caps are considered caring, laborers in their hard hats are considered strong, and graduates in their mortarboard caps are considered smart.

Discuss the possibility of children empowering themselves with strengths and skills by creating and wearing Power Hats. For example, the children could create any of the following hats:

Thinking Hats

Courage Hats

Caring Hats

Comfort Hats

Respect Hats

Contented Hats

No-More-Anger Hats

Cooperation Hats

Have the children choose a hat title. Ask them to think about what they need to make themselves feel like the hat title they have chosen. What might they need or want in order to feel courageous, respected, and so forth.

Suggest children draw a hat with the symbolic items that would help them feel stronger or safer, or use the photocopies of hats you have drawn. Younger children can describe the hat to you and you can draw it.

The children could make hats out of paper, glitter, scraps, etc. They may wear their hats when they feel it is appropriate.

Magic Camera

Procedure

Talk about how people see their world, their viewpoint, and how our memories are like pictures in our mind.

Introduce cameras by explaining how the person using the camera controls what they see or do not see. Discuss how the children can use the camera as a "safe window" to see things that might be too scary to look at directly. With the camera, the child can choose to turn off a scene or look at something different. A camera lens allows a child to view a scene without being part of it.

Discuss what some of these scary images might be: fierce animals, dark basements, dark closets, dark streets, or emergency rooms.

Encourage the children to look through the magazines, or the photos you have cut out, to find pictures that are scary to them. Ask the children to use or look through the camera viewfinder and think about how it makes them feel to see a scene but not be in it. Does it make them feel safer, stronger, or more courageous?

Variations

Encourage the children to use their imaginations and draw private pictures of experiences or memories that are scary. Then have them draw a second picture of how they might change that memory by looking at it through a magic camera. Discuss with the children how they might be able to change or create alternative memories or viewpoints without the camera by using their imaginations.

Suggestions

Read the book *If I Ran the Family*, by Lee Kaiser Johnson and Sue Kaiser Johnson (Free Spirit Publishing, 1992).

Issues

Powerlessness.

Purpose

To provide an opportunity for children to control what they see.

Materials

Old cameras (without film), paper, crayons or pencils, photocopies of the paper frames you draw yourself, and a selection of magazine photos or magazines.

ACTIVITY 33

Heart Healer

Issues

Physical or emotional insecurity, rejection, powerlessness.

Purpose

To help children develop and trust their personal strengths.

Materials

The children's book *Sofia and the Heartmenders* by Marie Olofsdotter (Free Spirit Publishing, 1993), drawing paper, markers or crayons, and a business-size envelope.

Procedure

Read *Sofia and the Heartmenders*. Discuss shadow-monsters and any insights the children learned from the story. Talk about whether it might be helpful for children to create an imaginary Heart Healer for themselves.

Encourage the children to imagine the sort of person who would make a good Heart Healer for them or another child they know in real life or from TV. What special qualities would this Heart Healer have? Are there any special tools or resources this Heart Healer would carry?

Ask them to draw the Heart Healer they have imagined.

Suggestions

Discuss the possibility of drawing Heart Healers who could bring a message of comfort and hope to children with special needs. What children might like to receive such a drawing and message? You might suggest a local children's hospital or homeless shelter. Offer envelopes to the children who want to mail their Heart Healers. Stuff, seal, and collect the envelopes. Mail these only after making arrangements with a staff person at the designated hospital or shelter.

Toolbox for Fixing the World

Issues
Hopelessness, powerlessness.

Purpose
To empower children and help them build a sense of their future.

Materials
Drawing paper and markers or crayons.

Procedure

Discuss what might make the world a better place. What needs to be fixed to build a world fit for children? Encourage the children to think symbolically when considering what tools would be needed to fix the world. Make a list of tools on the blackboard. If the children need guidance, offer the following suggestions: a file to smooth the rough edges, a rubber hammer to pound out the dents, a paint brush for a shiny new look, or a broom to sweep away yet another thing. Be sure to guide them toward constructive outcomes.

Suggestions

Have the children draw a toolbox and the tools they would select to make the world a better place for children.

Tongue Depressor Puppets

Issues

Disempowerment.

Purpose

To provide opportunities for children to rework situations and create more favorable endings.

Materials

Tongue depressors, colored construction paper, fabric or yarn, markers or crayons, and a stapler or glue.

Procedure

Do as a follow-up to a book the group read together or a video they watched that has a favorable ending. Have children make tongue depressor puppets of the characters. Encourage them to create different storylines and endings for the book or video.

This activity is also good for special times when a tragic community or national event occurs, such as a fire, earthquake, or terrorist attack, and all the children are aware of it. Discuss the characters the children would like to include and the roles they would like to play. The following are some suggested characters:

Police officers	Athletes
Emergency medical persons	Family members
Doctors	Neighbors
Nurses	Clergy
Social Workers	Playmates

Suggestions

Encourage the children to work in groups and create complex scripts such as the puppet scripts in chapter six.

ACTIVITY 36

Building Dreams

Procedure

This can be a group or individual activity. Encourage the children to build a school, hospital, playground, or backyard of their dreams, using these materials. Remind them to create one in which they might feel safe, happy, and successful.

Encourage them to draw pictures of any people they would like to have join them in their dream building. Have them draw pictures of what they would like the inside of the buildings to look like.

Suggestions

Encourage the children to list the activities they will do while they are there. Have them compose letters inviting anyone they wish to their dream place.

Issues

Powerlessness, insecurity.

Purpose

To help children build their dream environments.

Materials

Building blocks; discarded boxes, tubes, spools, yarn; and pipe cleaners.

Designing
Cities of Hope

Issues
Powerlessness, insecurity.

Purpose
To help children design safe and hopeful cities.

Materials
A roll of brown wrapping paper and crayons or markers.

Procedure

Have the children divide into groups of four or five to design a City of Hope together. Each group gets a section of the brown paper. Have the groups draw a city block (or playground plan) in which they would feel safe and hopeful. Encourage them to think about where they could safely play or walk. Ask them to think about who would be in their city or playground to keep children safe. Suggest they include people in their drawing.

Ask each group to present their plan to the whole group.

ACTIVITY
38

Designing a Dream House

Issues

Powerlessness, insecurity.

Purpose

To help children design their dream homes.

Materials

Sheets of construction paper that are 14" x 17" inches, crayons or markers, rulers, yardsticks, pencils, and a sample house plan.

Procedure

Discuss the importance of dreams and the ability to think about our dreams whenever we want to. Give each child paper, markers and other materials necessary to design their dream house. Encourage the children to draw plans of a dream house that they can visit whenever they need to. Younger children can describe the floor plan to you. You can draw the floor plan. They can fill in the details.

Suggestions

Talk about safe places and how everyone needs such a place. Ask them how a person would know they are in a safe place. Ask them how a safe place would feel to them. Then have them look at their dream house. Is there a safe place for them there? How could they change their plan to include such a place?

ACTIVITY 39

The Powerful Beat

Procedure

Ask if anyone knows why some families place a ticking clock next to their new puppies, especially at night. Discuss how the ticking of the clock reminds the puppy of the sound of the mother dog's heartbeat, so the puppy does not feel as lonely.

Listen to a recording of the human heartbeat. Ask if anyone knows why recordings of heartbeats are placed into teddy bears or other baby toys. Do babies need comforting just like puppies do? Ask what feelings they have while listening to the heartbeat.

Listen to recordings of different drum music. Ask the children how they feel when they listen to the music. Discuss their responses and talk about when such recordings might be comforting and relaxing to hear. Do different beat speeds or tempos cause people to feel something different?

Introduce percussion instruments to the children, such as drums, rattles, or sticks. Pass out the instruments. Ask the children to demonstrate on the various instruments a beat or tempo they find comforting and relaxing. Discuss other feelings generated by drums—for the drummer and for the listener. For example, a fast drum beat might be exciting for the listener but exhausting for the player.

Discuss ways the children could improvise to create a healing beat or tempo when they need it to comfort themselves. One example might be a ticking clock in their room at night or the hum of a fan.

Issues

Insecurity, feeling disconnected, loneliness.

Purpose

To help children feel secure and connected to the people and places around them.

Materials

Recording of human heart beats, or a teddy bear designed for infants with such a recording inside, tape recordings of African and American Indian drumming, and percussion instruments.

Body Language

Procedure

Discuss what is meant by body language and how we can show feelings without words. Put on the music. Ask the children to move around the room in rhythm, being respectful of each other's space, with the music playing. After they have warmed up, tell them you will call out a behavior, or an action people do or express, and you want them to show the behavior. Instruct them to use their entire body for the movement, including their head, arms, trunk, and legs, but not to use words, sounds, or their voice at all. Allow several minutes between naming behaviors. The following are some examples of behaviors you might use:

Blaming	Protecting
Caring	Punishing
Comforting	Resisting
Controlling	Scaring
Coughing	Screaming
Crying	Singing
Hiding	Smiling
Hurting	Telling
Laughing	Threatening
Listening	Yelling
Loving	

Issues

Limited body and impulse control, powerlessness.

Purpose

To express feelings in ways other than words.

Materials

Recorded marches, dance music, or dream music.

Silently Stepping Forward

Issues

Powerlessness, insecurity.

Purpose

To help children understand and appreciate their ability to be brave and act on their own feelings.

Materials

Tape recordings of African and American Indian drumming.

Procedure

Ask the children to move around the room, imitating the image and behavior of the animals you will call out. Encourage them to use their entire bodies—arms, face, trunk, legs, and feet. Ask that they make no sounds but communicate the suggested animal image with their bodies and their walking styles. Ask that they respect the safety and space of their classmates or friends.

Explain those animals the children may not be familiar with before the activity begins. Allow the children at least two or more minutes to fully express the symbolic walking action before calling out the next animal. Remind them to be silent, as needed.

Here are some suggested animal identities:

Angry Alligator	Limping Leopard
Bellowing Buffalo	Mad Monster
Brave Bear	Nasty Night Owl
Courageous Cheetah	Obstinate Ostrich
Dancing Deer	Puffing Panther
Dangerous Dragon	Quarreling Quail
Elegant Elk	Roaring Raccoon
Fierce Feline	Slithering Snake
Foxy Fox	Treacherous Tiger
Graceful Giraffe	Unlovable Unicorn
Happy Hippo	Vivacious Vulture
Incredible Insect	Wacky Walrus
Insolent Ibex	Whimpering Weasel
Jolly Jaguar	Yelping Yak
Karate Kangaroo	Zany Zebra
Laughing Llama	

After going through the list of animals, listen to the drum recordings of different tempos. Play them again and ask the children to match an animal style with the beat or tempo being played. Repeat with different tempos as interest allows.

ACTIVITY

42

The Screaming Beat

Issues

Powerlessness, limited impulse control.

Purpose

To show children how to release energy and regain control of themselves.

Materials

A musical instrument, such as a piano or drum, or a tape recording of drumming music.

Procedure

Play drum recordings or instruments and encourage the children to move around the room, repeating their own name in beat with the music. As you increase and decrease the volume and tempo, encourage the children to match their voice volume, body movements, and energy to the music.

Repeat this activity, having the children use the name and sound of an animal instead of their names.

Be prepared to reinforce safety guidelines and awareness for all children. Slow the tempo and volume as needed. Provide calming comfort as needed.

Mr. and Ms. Body Language

Issues

Powerlessness, poor body image, physical insecurity, feelings of shame.

Purpose

To provide children with a healthy opportunity to validate their own bodies, feelings, and personal space.

Materials

Recorded music of various tempos and styles.

Procedure

Play music of differing tempos and styles to the children. While the music is playing, encourage the children to think of their entire bodies as "making" similar music, sending messages into the space around them through their body language while matching their body movement to the expressions of the music.

Suggest the children imagine their bodies are magic instruments that can scribble the music's message into the spaces around them. Caution them about respecting the space and safety of each other.

ACTIVITY 44

Working Our Feelings Out

Issues

Powerlessness, physical insecurity, feelings of shame.

Purpose

To support children in learning that feelings are expressed by their entire body.

Materials

Masking tape, plain paper plates, and markers.

Procedure

Before the children arrive, draw faces showing different feelings on the paper plates. You will need two plates for each feeling. Tape one set of plates on the wall at a height children can reach.

Hand out the other set of plates randomly to the children. One at a time, have the children define and describe their feeling plate. Then have the child walk or dramatically move through the room in a style that demonstrates the feeling face. The children end by finding the plate on the wall that matches theirs. Be sure to applaud or otherwise affirm each child's enactment.

Speaking Hands

Procedure

Discuss how we can communicate with our entire bodies or with our hands alone. Ask the children to pick a partner, then sit on the floor closely facing each other. Ask them to shake hands with their partner. Then ask them to describe how it felt. Was it warm, cold, firm, soft, energized, or relaxed?

Next, direct them to shake hands in a way that communicates specific ideas such as confidence and then gentleness. Ask them how they could tell which was which. What were the clues?

Ask one partner to communicate one of the following feelings by the way she uses her hands to touch her partner's hands. Have the partners reverse roles.

Suggested feelings to communicate:

Caring

Excitement

Friendship

Frustration

Happiness

Joy

Loneliness

Sadness

Tenderness

Ask the children how they could tell which way to shake or use their hands or how they could tell what feeling their partner was communicating. Repeat as desired.

Issues
Insecurity, lack of trust.

Purpose
To support children in learning to trust their own intuition, feelings, and bodies.

Materials
Floor space and tapes of soothing music.

ACTIVITY
46

Dancing Hands, Bodies, and Feet

Issues

Physical insecurity, poor body image, lack of self-control, and lack of trust.

Purpose

To help children gain confidence and self-control through physically leading and following others.

Materials

Music with a relaxing, steady beat and floor space.

Procedure

Ask the children to pick a partner, then kneel facing each other. Each pair should choose who will lead first. Instruct the first leaders to make a variety of hand movements and the partners to mirror those hand movements. Remind partners not to touch or interfere with each other's movement. Stop the music and have the children change roles. Discuss whether this was easy or hard to do. Did it feel comfortable or uneasy leading someone? Following someone? Which was easier?

Ask the children to stand up and repeat the activity but add full arm, head, and trunk movements. Stop the music and have the children change roles. Discuss whether they feel more in control or safe when following or leading. Ask them what helped them feel comfortable when they mirrored their partner.

Ask the children to repeat the activity but this time using their entire body for the movements, including, for example, feet and lips. The children should be instructed to stay within one basic space. They should also be reminded to respect each other's body space. Stop the music and have the children change roles. Discuss whether they are more or less comfortable using their whole body. Is it more or less difficult to feel safe and secure when using your entire body?

Cradling Arms

Issues

Emotional insecurity, feeling unloved, poor caregiving skills.

Purpose

To help children learn to trust themselves and others by giving and receiving care.

Materials

Recorded lullabies.

Procedure

Listen to lullabies and discuss the feelings they generate. Sing some favorites together. Ask the children if they liked to be rocked when they were younger. Why? How did it make them feel? Is rocking like cradling?

Ask the children to form teams of three each. Pick three teams of three to start (nine children). The remaining children form a large circle around them. Ask two children from each team (six children) to form a cradle by sitting on the floor facing each other with their legs crossed. You will have three cradles, each formed by two children. Ask the remaining children to carefully enter their individual team cradle, without stepping on anyone, and sit down inside it in a position that is comfortable for all.

Play the recording of the lullabies and encourage the children cradling to rock gently to comfort and protect the "baby." Have the children in the circle help sing the lullaby as softly and lovingly as they can as they watch.

For each round of activity, you set the scenario. Here are some examples:

A lonely child needs rocking.

A baby robin is in a nest during a wind storm.

A baby panda bear is feeling ill.

A baby chimp has fallen from a branch and needs comforting.

Encourage the "baby" in the cradle to make appropriate sound effects such as whimpering or peeping noises. Repeat the activity to accommodate other children as needed.

ACTIVITY 48

Body Power

Procedure

Encourage children to use their hands as instruments of healing by slowly, gently moving their hands around their own bodies from head to feet without touching. Ask them to imagine they are sending themselves warm, healing energy. Encourage them to concentrate on the areas of their bodies that may especially need this healing warmth and to receive it with joy and gratitude. Allow plenty of time for the children to think, feel, and sense this activity.

Ask interested children to move close to another child and gently give this warm, healing energy to one another. Reassure those not interested in working with another child to stand back and not participate in teams. Encourage them to continue the activity by themselves. Tell all the children to move with the music. Discuss the activity. Ask if the children could feel the warmth using their imaginations and if it made anyone feel comfortable.

Issues

Powerlessness, limited impulse control.

Purpose

To provide opportunities for children to send healing energy to themselves and others.

Materials

Any recorded soothing music, such as Pachelbel's *Canon,* Vivaldi's *Summer* or Brahms *Lullaby*; and floor space. (Please note, this activity is a good complement to activity forty-five.)

ACTIVITY 49

Stroking Gently

Procedure

Discuss different kinds of touches such as comfortable touches, uncomfortable touches and comforting touches. List the different touches on a chalkboard or large paper if age-appropriate. Explain to the children that everyone has the right to choose what kind of touch to give and receive. Affirm that we all have the ability to make choices. At any time during this activity, be sure to allow any child to not participate.

Discuss which kinds of touches we would like to receive, which ones we would like to share with others, and which ones we wish would never happen to anyone. Ask what kinds of emotions we feel when we receive gentle caring touches on our arms or faces. Could giving gentle caring touches bring those same feelings?

Tell the children to choose a partner. Have one partner sit relaxed on the floor with eyes closed. The other partner kneels close behind. Tell the kneeling child to gently stroke the partner's face, cheeks, and neck, while very gently swaying their partner's head in rhythm with the music. After several minutes, ask the giving children to move their hands to gently stroke the receiving child's shoulders and upper back. Ask the receiving child to be aware of the comforting warmth being given through the gentle strokes and touching. Encourage the child to freely absorb and receive the healing comfort.

After several minutes, ask the stroking child to place his hands at his side and feel the comforting warmth that passed between them.

Discuss what it felt like to be the receiver of the comforting touches. Did they feel warmth or coldness? Safe or unsafe? What did it feel like to be the giver of the gentle strokes? Caring or uncaring? Strong or weak? Accepted or rejected? Have the partners switch places and repeat the exercise and discussion.

Issues

Low tolerance for risk taking, lack of trust, emotional insecurity.

Purpose

To help children learn to trust themselves and others.

Materials

Any recorded soothing music, such as Pachelbel's *Canon*, Vivaldi's *Summer* or Brahms *Lullaby*.

Giving Friendship Gifts

Issues

Insecurity, feeling unloved or unwanted, poor care-giving skills.

Purpose

To help children learn to trust themselves and others by giving and receiving care.

Materials

Recorded soothing music with a steady, even tempo.

Procedure

Talk about giving friendship and affection. What makes it possible for a person to give and receive gifts of friendship? How do trusting and liking yourself, and being happy and worry-free fit in? Can anyone ever have too much affection or friendship? Too little?

Ask the children to choose a partner and sit on the floor, facing each other with their legs crossed, so that their knees almost touch. Ask one partner to pick an imaginary, valuable gift out of the air or from behind them and give it, gently and lovingly, to their partner. Ask them to "speak" only with their eyes and face and use no words or sounds.

Encourage the receiving partners to accept the gift with delight and sincerity, demonstrating their joy through their gentle, receiving hands and glowing faces. After communicating this appreciation, ask the receivers to place the imaginary gift gently on the floor near them. Play soothing music during the activity. Have the children reverse their roles and repeat the activity.

Guide the children in a discussion of their experiences and their feelings. The following are some questions to ask: How did you feel as you received the gift? Did it matter that it was only an imaginary gift? What about the gift made you feel cared for and valued? How did you feel when you gave the gift? Did it bother you to give an invisible gift? Could you sense the receiver appreciated your gift? How could you tell that?

Allow them to share the identity of the gifts, if they would like.

6 Healing Language Arts

Guided Language Arts

Language arts provide meaningful healing opportunities for pre-school, elementary, or middle school students. At the same time, language arts can expand and strengthen a progam or school's established educational goals. By outlining specific goals and challenges for creative writing, you can provide children with a constructive way to relieve themselves from personal stress and anxieties, through fictional characters.

Preschool children who have not yet developed (or children who have underdeveloped) writing skills can participate in creative literary activities through dictation. Based on your familiarity with the children, assign teams where one child records the unfolding story while the other "reporters" dictate. Teacher aides or student mentors might be alternative recorders. All recorders must understand that taking dictation means only asking judgement-free questions for clarification purposes. Individual or group story-telling can also offer an alternative format for children who do not yet write or who find writing stressful. Young children can also draw their stories and tell you, or not tell you about them. You can suggest children read their stories to the group only after you have read all the submissions to determine whether or not any poten-tially damaging or intensely private issues are included.

The personal meanings behind such creative writings must remain private and confidential unless the child chooses to elabo-rate or share. Creative writing assignments are never to be used to get information. It is essential for you to remember that when children are offered opportunities to explore and express their feel-ings, needs, and beliefs through creative writing, neither the story line nor the child can be judged or criticized. Whenever children are encouraged to disclose their personal perspectives or intuitive senses through literary activities, the philosophical or moral con-tent must remain free of evaluation or comment.

The key to empowerment is the process, not the final literary product. Children can heal vicariously as they become connected to a character in their story, working through the same or similar experiences and feelings. You may not even be aware when or if children are using the assignment as a healing exercise. The child engaged in the cathartic process may not even be aware of it.

As indicated earlier, healing breakthroughs can get rid of accumulated negative energy. This may result in immediate behavioral changes for some children. You are encouraged to view this as a natural outcome and not a discipline issue. If acting-out behaviors become prolonged, then consider referral. (See the appendix for more information about referrals.)

Whenever tragic local or national events are featured extensively in the media, you might consider introducing one of the creative writing activities from this chapter or create one that suits the circumstances. They can apply to natural disasters like earthquakes or tornadoes, accidents, or deliberate acts of violence. Recognizing that anxieties may not surface for six to eight months following an ordeal, consider introducing an additional literary activity at a later time or periodically as part of your teaching.

The cathartic potential of literary activities can be reinforced by encouraging the authors to illustrate their stories.

(No additional materials are needed unless otherwise noted.)

ACTIVITY 51

Power Lists

Procedure

Discuss the idea of wish lists. Affirm with children their ability to empower themselves by choosing to have strong, helping thoughts and feelings for themselves. Have the children make lists about how they could help themselves in the following ways:

To feel safer

To feel hopeful

To feel less lonely

To feel respected

To feel happier

This exercise needs to be judgment-free, but the children need to understand that all answers or items should not bring harm to self, others, or property.

Issues

Loss, stress, loneliness, fear, powerlessness.

Purpose

To help children affirm their choices and recognize their personal power.

ACTIVITY
52

Letters from the Heart

Procedure

Suggest to the children that they write letters to one or more of the following:

A person who could be their secret friend

Their own angel

The hero of their choice

A person they would like to have appear in their dreams

An animal they would like to have appear in their dreams

An animal they would choose as their friend

Variations

For younger children with fewer or no writing skills, have them dictate individual letters or a group letter that you write down.

Issues

Powerlessness, physical and emotional insecurity, low self-esteem.

Purpose

To help children develop hope, a sense of security, and trust.

ACTIVITY 53

Secret Messages

Issues

Powerlessness, physical insecurity, loneliness.

Purpose

To help children develop hope, security, and trust.

Materials

Stationery and envelopes.

Procedure

Provide the children with stationery. Ask them to write a note based on the following questions:

If a bird (or a lion, wolf, or butterfly) offered to deliver a special, secret message for you, what type of bird would you choose?

What would the message say?

To whom or where would it be delivered?

Would it be sung or delivered as a note?

After the notes are written, have the children decorate their stationery. Pass out the envelopes. Ask them to place their messages in envelopes, seal them, and place the envelopes in a special box you provide. Assure them that the envelopes will not be opened by anyone because an imaginary animal is guarding the note and will keep it safe. Honor that promise.

You can ask preschool children or children with limited writing skills the question, and they can draw pictures for answers or they can dictate their answers to a writer.

Cuddly Cartoons

Issues

Insecurity, loneliness, loss, fear.

Purpose

To help children develop hope by learning how to resolve problems.

Materials

A sheet of paper, a black marker, and access to a photocopier.

Procedure

Before the children arrive draw a frame on the paper with the black marker. Make as many copies as you will need depending on whether you will have the children work individually or as teams. Instruct the children, whether working individually or in teams, to create a cartoon strip using six of the photocopied frames. Younger children can draw wordless cartoons or draw one large, frameless mural. Suggest they create a cuddly cartoon about a baby animal that deals with any of the following issues:

feeling lonely

getting lost

feeling sad about the loss of someone or something

feeling angry

feeling scared

being kind and caring

Variations

Consider offering the first frame complete with drawings and script and the second frame with just the drawing. Leave the remaining frames blank for the children to complete.

ACTIVITY 55

Power Comics

Issues

Powerlessness, fear, vulnerability.

Purpose

To help empower children through positive thinking and caring.

Materials

Optional laminating materials.

Procedure

Suggest the children create six block comic strips or cartoon booklets that include at least one of the following:

power finders

power thinkers

power fixers

power helpers

power protectors

power friends

Tell the children that all powers are to be positive powers. Children design the models for their power characters. Discuss the importance of writing a story that involves a constructive resolution that respects all the characters and their safety rights.

Younger children could create a group cartoon or dictate to you the story or words to accompany their illustrations.

Variations

Depending on your resources, bind and laminate these cartoons into permanent comic books and have an author's party.

Issues

Powerlessness, insecurity, anger, sadness, fear.

Purpose

To help teach children constructive skills for managing anger, sadness, powerlessness, insecurity, and fear.

Kid Town Commercials

Procedure

Have the children divide into journalistic teams. Explain that your role of editor will be to guide the commercial production to insure its quality and eventual use. Instruct the teams to write a script for a TV commercial or public service announcement. The script can be acted out or drawn as a cartoon commercial. Suggest the following topics:

Inform children they have a right to be safe.

Inform girls they have a right to show anger and show how to use anger constructively.

Inform children they have a right to say "No" to someone who will not respect their health or safety.

Show how to deal constructively with put-downs.

Inform boys they can be sad and show how to express it.

Inform boys they can be caring and show how to express it.

Inform children that fear is normal and show how to use intuition to stay safe.

Suggestions

After writing the commercial, produce it. Visit a TV studio.

Puppet Scripts

Procedure

Have the children divide into teams that are a comfortable size for them and for you. Each team will work together to write or dictate and then perform puppet scripts about one of the following ideas:

A. There is a lion cub who did not pay attention when his aunt, the leader of the pride, was giving a lesson on how to hide in the tall grass for safety. Now the cub doesn't know what to do or how to do it and has to ask directions. Whom does he ask? How does he learn what he needs to know? When and where does he practice? How does he feel at the beginning of the story and at the end?

B. There is a little squirrel in a family of three who always gets blamed for whatever has gone wrong. How does this feel for her? How does she figure out what she might do about this? How does she figure out what she chooses to do and what not to do? Whom does she talk with about this? What advice does she give her younger cousin about avoiding or resolving a similar situation?

C. There is a little puppy who feels lost and lonely and doesn't have anyone he can depend on. What does he do to find himself a person he can depend on? Where does he look? Whom does he talk to? How does he decide whom to choose and whom not to choose? How does he feel at the beginning of the story and at the end?

D. There is a dragon who is burning up with anger and cannot let off steam through her nostrils because she has a cold. How does she figure out how to release her hot, angry feelings so they won't be so uncomfortable for her? How does she do this and not hurt anyone or anything else? How does she feel at the beginning of the story and at the end?

E. There is a tiger cub who has to figure out a way to turn fear into bravery as he deals with a crocodile. What does he say to himself to think it through? How does he build his courage? How does he decide what to do and what not to do?

F. There is a kitten who has climbed very high into a tree and doesn't know how to get down safely. She is told by one relative to do it one way and by another relative to do it another. What kinds of directions might they have given her? How does she think through the advice and decide for herself what she can do? How does she get down? What does she decide about whom she will trust in the future when she is safely down and discussing this with her grandmother?

Issues

Powerlessness, loss, anger, feeling rejected.

Purpose

To help children learn to express and deal with feelings and to generate solutions to problems.

G. There is a young raccoon who has just awakened from a nap and is hungry. On his way to his favorite garbage can he hears a baby raccoon crying because he is lost, wet, and cold. The young raccoon first decides to ignore the lost baby and go on to the garbage can, but then stops and turns back to help the baby. What might he have thought to himself? How did he help the baby? Did he need any help? If so, whom did he get to help him? How did he feel about himself at the end?

H. There is a young rabbit who has much sadness and many worries. How does she get to feel better? How does she figure out what to do? Whom does she talk with? Whom does she decide not to talk with? Why? What does she say to herself and to others? What does she do for herself to feel better? How does she feel about herself at the end? What does she decide she can do for herself so she will not feel so sad and worried in the future?

I. There is a puppy who is separated from his mommy. While he is walking around looking for her, he discovers things that remind him of her. How does he use his imagination and the memories he discovers to lessen his sadness and his loneliness? What does he connect with his memory of how warm and safe he felt when she snuggled him? What reminded him of her smell, her voice, the sound of her tail, or the feel of her hair? How did he turn these memories into comforting feelings for himself?

J. There is a kitten in the house alone who hears a loud scary sound. How does the kitten feel? What does she say to herself? How does she decide to do something about her own safety? What is her safety plan? How does the kitten feel about the plan? How does the plan work? How does she feel when she has finished her plan?

K. There is a doll that is sick and taken to the doll hospital. How does the doll feel when he sees the rooms and equipment? What do the caring doctors and nurses do for the doll? How does he start to feel better? How does the child who loves the doll feel when he is retrieved home safe and healthy? How does the doll feel?

L. There is a kitten whose mother has adopted a lost little bunny that wandered into their yard. How does the kitten feel when the bunny snuggled up to the kitten's mom? And when mom licked the bunny? Did the kitten feel confusion? If so, why? How did she decide to tell her mom what she was feeling? How did the mom cat respond? How did the mom and the kitten heal their differences? What happened between the kitten and the bunny?

M. There is a bear family—Mama, Papa, and Baby—who live in the woods. One day Papa Bear packed everything he had into his suitcases, shouted "I'm leaving," and slammed the door. How did

Baby Bear feel? How did Baby Bear decide what to do next? What did Baby Bear decide to do next? How did Baby Bear start to deal with his feelings? Whom does Baby Bear decide to tell his feelings to? How does this help Baby Bear?

N. There is a baby lamb whose mother didn't like her and didn't pay attention to her. How did the lamb feel? What did she do to try to win acceptance by her mother? How does the lamb decide she needs to find a substitute mother? What did the lamb do to begin this process? Whom did the lamb talk to about her needs?

O. There is a dog who wants to join a pack of dogs but is not the same color as any of the other dogs. He does not recognize or feel comfortable with any of them. Explain how he decides to introduce himself. What does he decide to say or not say? What does he decide to do or not do so the other dogs could feel more comfortable? Describe how he thinks this through for himself.

People Puppets

Issues

Insecurity with gender or feelings.

Purpose

To give children opportunities to become comfortable with gender and feelings that may not fit cultural stereotypes.

Procedure

List the following characters on paper or the board:

<u>Characters</u>

Frustrated Freddie

Protector Paula

Tearful Todd

Cooperative Charlie

Powerful Petula

Precious Paul

Courageous Caroline

Anxious Andy

Cautious Chris

Helpful Harry

Hassling Heather

Troublesome Tabatha

Loving Leon

(Choose names that match children's environment and culture.)

Encourage the children to select and write one puppet script, using one of these characters to resolve the issues listed here:

<u>Issues</u>

How do friends or classmates show their expectations of behaviors for the title character?

How does the title character respond to these expectations?

How does the title character decide to believe in himself?

How does the title character let others know that she is proud of herself?

With your guidance, younger children can make up a story and act it out with the puppets that show that both boys and girls can be and express themselves in many different ways.

The Lonely Monster

Issues

Loneliness, feeling rejected, powerlessness.

Purpose

To help children learn to make friends.

Procedure

Have the children write or dictate a story about a lonely monster. Include things such as how a lonely monster without friends tries to make friends but is rejected.

Describe his thinking process for discovering what friends might want from him. What makes potential friends feel uncomfortable around him? Describe how he chooses what type of a friend he wants to be. What does he do to get to know others whom he could be friends with and would want as his friends?

Variation

With your guidance, younger children can make up a story and act it out with the puppets.

Taming Nightmares

Issues

Fears, flashbacks or nightmares, powerlessness.

Purpose

To help children learn to trust in themselves and cope with their fears.

Procedure

Have the children write a story about a child who has bad dreams and decides how to tame the monsters in the nightmares and make them less scary.

Describe how the child thinks this through. What are the possible problems? How are the dreams processed and how does the child feel at each stage? When the child feels confident the bad dreams have been tamed, whom does the child share the experience of success with and celebrate the joy with?

Variation

Read *The Adventures of Isabel* by Ogden Nash (Little, Brown and Company, 1991) with the children. Discuss how Isabel deals with her dreams.

The Secret

Procedure

Have the children write an adventure story about a child who has gone to a place he was told not to go alone. While there, the child sees something happen that is so scary the child decides not to tell anyone about it. Describe how the child feels in body and mind. The child wants to forget the event but the secret memory keeps coming back. Tell how the child tries to keep from remembering. Describe the thinking process he uses to decide the secret needs to be shared. How does the child select the person to tell? How does he feel after sharing the secret?

Issues

Fear from flashbacks, powerlessness.

Purpose

To help children clarify their reasoning and affirm their feelings and options.

A Safety Plan

Procedure

Discuss feeling safe and feeling unsafe. How could a child know or sense when unsafe places may be near? Explain what intuition is by relating it to how someone feels when they hear creepy music start to play in a movie or on TV.

Have the children write, draw, or tell a story about a child who fears loud noise because it brings back a bad memory and tells the child she is no longer safe. Describe the thinking process and self-talk process that led the child to believe she was not safe. Have the children outline the words or messages the scared child says to herself to help her do something about her own safety. Describe her complete safety plan, thinking about where, when, and how. Describe the child's feelings about herself when she has created a sense of security.

Suggestions

Have the children who write the story illustrate it with a complete floor plan as part of the safety plan.

Issues

Fear, powerlessness.

Purpose

To empower children by helping them expand their problem-solving skills.

ACTIVITY 63

Sad Tales

Procedure

Have the children write, draw, or tell a story about a child who finds a baby kitten who is obviously not healthy and strong.

Describe how the child tenderly cares for the baby kitten until it dies after a week. Describe the child's confusion and anger over why something so small and helpless dies. What does he say to himself? Are there any "what ifs" he might think about? How does he express or act out his angry feelings? Describe how he decides what is anger and what is sadness and how to relieve those feelings. What does he choose to do about his angry and sad feelings? Describe how the child chooses to share his feelings with someone he trusts. How does the child decide who that person might be? Describe any actions the child and the person he talks to may choose to do to resolve or complete the grieving process.

Issues

Loss, grief.

Purpose

To provide children with a way to affirm and process their feelings of loss or grief.

ACTIVITY 64

Lonesome Tales

Issues

Loss, separation, loneliness, anger.

Purpose

To help children see the connection between grief and anger and recognize positive choices.

Procedure

Have the children write, draw, or tell a story about a child who is feeling very sad because a family member the child loves is no longer a part of the family or available to the child. The child also feels bad—angry and rejected.

Describe how she feels. Because the child feels bad she does something uncaring and hurtful. How could feeling bad lead to feeling angry and wanting to hurt something or someone? Describe the thinking process and what the child says silently to herself. Describe how the child figures out how to manage the angry feelings and release them without hurting herself, others, or property.

The Magic Trunk

Issues

Powerlessness, fear, insecurity.

Purpose

To empower children by making them aware of their choices.

Procedure

Have the children write, draw or tell a story about a child who finds a magic trunk filled with special clothes or costumes and accessories or props.

On the trunk lid are written directions that say, "Choose Who or What You Wish To Be. Reach Into the Trunk and You Will Find a Set of Clothes that Will Turn You Into That Person." Instruct the children to pick what or whom they want the child to be. Describe what the clothes and props would look like. Describe how the child who wears them feels. Describe what the child will now be able to do. Describe what now needs to be done. Describe how the child now feels about him or herself and how others around the child respond. Is the child treated differently than before? Encourage the children to give the story a positive ending.

Suggestions

Illustrate the story or make it into a puppet script or a play.

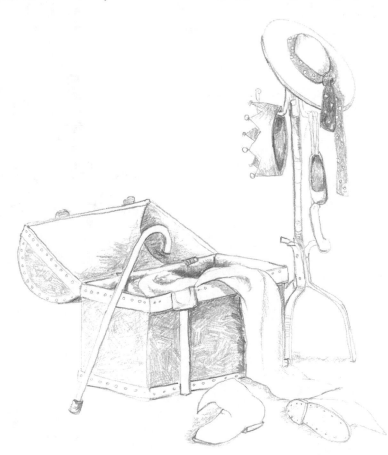

ACTIVITY 66

A Friend in Need

Issues

Insecurity, loneliness.

Purpose

To help children learn alternative sources for caring and stability.

Procedure

Have the children write a story about a child who feels lonely and insecure and wants to be cared for in a stable environment.

How does the child feel? How does the child decide he has a right to feel secure and to be cared for? Describe the thought process and what the child said to himself. How does the child decide he will find someone who will be a caring friend to him? Outline how the child decided where to find this caring person and how he selected the person. Tell about the very first experience they shared together and how the child felt. Describe how the child is looking forward to the future now that there is more stability and caring in his life.

Comfort Zones

Issues

Stress, fears, insecurity.

Purpose

To help children manage their stress and fears while building a sense of security.

Procedure

Have the children write, draw or tell a story about a child who has just transferred to a new school or child care center and is finding the experience stressful and lonely.

Describe how the child feels about the new setting. Is it hard to go to the new place each morning? Suppose the child tries to make friends with a group of children at lunch and she is rejected and made fun of. How will she deal with this and find another place to sit?

Describe how the child feels as she goes home that afternoon and begins to daydream about her dream school or center. What would her dream school or center be like? How do the adults and children treat new children? What might they say and do differently? Is there one place in the dream school or center where the child feels especially safe and comfortable? Who else might come to that place? What does the child think about and say to herself to make it possible for her to feel comfortable about returning the next day?

Broken Wing— Broken Dreams

Issues

Loneliness, hopelessness.

Purpose

To affirm needs for hope and a future and to honor the strengths of free spirits.

Procedure

Have the children write, draw or tell a story about a child who finds a hawk or pigeon with a broken wing. (Please note, children who tend to have behavior outbursts usually relate well to the wild spirit of a hawk.)

Ask the children to describe how the child decides to help the injured bird. What is the bird's reactions to the child's approach and handling? How does the child feel while trying to help the bird? How will the child care for the bird? What specific things does he do for the bird? Why does he do these things? What might the child say to himself as he provides care and comfort for the bird? How do his family and friends respond to the bird and the child's caring for it? How does the child feel about their responses? What does he say to himself about their responses? How does the bird respond to the child as the care and healing progress? How does the child feel as this is happening? How does the story end? What happens to the bird? How does the child feel about the outcome for himself and the bird?

Suggestions

Contact your local natural history museum or zoo to learn who in your area is licensed to care for injured wild animals. Arrange, if possible, to have them bring an injured bird or other small animal to your classroom.

Star Bright—Star Power

Procedure

Have the children write, draw or tell a bedtime story about a child who finds great comfort in looking at her own special star at night through the window near her bed.

Describe what the special star looks like, for example, its colors or the way it sparkles. How does the child know which star is the special star? As the light from the star comes through the window into the bedroom, describe its special qualities, such as its colors or temperature. What does the star do for the child? What is their relationship? How does the child talk with or send messages to the star? How does the child decide what she wants or needs from the star? How does the child feel as the starlight wraps around her? What can the child now do, thanks to the special strength the star has given her?

Issues
Powerlessness, loneliness.

Purpose
To help children develop their self-empowerment skills.

7 Building Resiliency in Children

Providing the Tools for Children's Resiliency

It is unlikely that children's lives will ever be free from all chaos and violence, as much as we would like that to happen. How can we build resiliency in children to help them cope with possible tragic or frightening experiences? What kinds of skills will children need, to withstand the insults and assaults they might encounter?

Resilient children are able to maintain an excitement about life and live in the present. They are not restricted by the past or the future. Resilient children are capable of connecting with adults, including their teachers and caregivers, through bonds of mutual trust. They are self-reliant and believe in their own abilities and futures.

There are many ways for you to help children build resiliency. You can help them learn the following:

Express all their feelings

Manage their anger

Solve their problems

Manage their stress

Manage their fear

Manage their conflict

Participate in their own safety.

Expressing All Feelings

Probably the richest gift adults can give children is the ability to honor and trust all their feelings. This is the essential foundation that empowers children to use the energy of their feelings for positive resolutions. Before a child can develop skills for managing feelings, the feelings must be validated and affirmed. This is particularly important for children who have had experiences that taught them not to trust adults.

It is important to recognize the different implied messages about anger and fear that are given to children based on their gender. Many little girls have been taught that it is not nice to have angry feelings. As a result, they release their frustration with tears, which can reinforce their feelings of helplessness and be interpreted by others as powerlessness.

Boys often are taught that it is not masculine to feel sadness or fear. They may be told that those feelings are for "sissies." Your room or home may be the only place that boys can learn the strength involved in confronting fears and sadness and that girls can learn healthy ways to express anger. Their emotional health may depend on these learning opportunities.

Managing Anger

Children who have been given the right to honor and accept their feelings of anger are free to build skills for managing those feelings, as opposed to venting or acting them out. Suppressing anger is just as unhealthy. Children who are not shamed for their angry feelings can use those feelings to come up with solutions that build a sense of security and hope.

The most influential way you teach anger management is the way you manage your own anger. This is particularly true when you are responding to a child's anger or acting-out behavior.

Some children have learned, for survival purposes, that the only way to respond to another's anger is to react with their own. Some children may engage in inappropriate verbal or physical behavior in an attempt to cause the chaos with which they are familiar. This helps them feel normal and secure.

You can guide your children in rethinking and reworking their beliefs and behaviors by asking various questions:

I see you seem to be having angry feelings. Can you tell me what it feels like for you?

Would you like to be able to change how you are feeling?

How would you rather be feeling?

What might you do starting right now to make that possible?

Encouraging your children to release their anger through actions or exercise is another way to help them manage their behavior. There are many simple activities that can work:

Jumping rope

Stomping up and down the stairs

Stretching or exercising to music

Pounding pegs

Rhythmic movements such as dancing, stomping, and marching

Sports that do not involve direct physical contact, such as swimming, gymnastics, and martial arts.

Solving Problems

One way to build resiliency in children is to help them develop their problem-solving skills. Children who trust their problem-solving skills can face the uncertainties of their futures with greater self-confidence and hope.

Empowering children to brainstorm and generate alternative solutions requires that they trust the emotional security of their environment. They need to know they will not experience shame or humiliation. This is essential, whether the child is in a classroom, the hallway, a cafeteria, a car, a bus, a playground, a school office, or on a field trip. Having choices is paramount. If you do not provide children with choices, then their only option is obedience or disobedience. Obedience can bring perceptions of powerlessness to recovering children.

Connecting children with their hopes and dreams can motivate them to invest in a positive resolution rather than just placing blame. Blaming indicates that children do not know what to do next and feel powerless to create the change they may need.

You can guide the children toward solutions by asking open-ended questions:

What would you like to have happen differently?

What do you see happening that could make that possible?

What could you do to bring the change about?

Managing Stress

Uncertainty, pressure, and competition abound even for young children, from their home, school, and neighborhood. Some children place an inordinate amount of pressure on themselves for academic achievement. Others endure stress from their parents' expectations.

Tension and pressure can come from a child's sports, recreation, and entertainment—such as too much over-stimulating TV, movies, or video games. Loneliness is a significant factor in children's anxiety and stress. Some children's safety and very existence are at risk due to violence at home or in their community.

Children's worries need to be taken seriously, expressed, released, and resolved. This process can happen with children in your care only when they trust you. Structure and predictability can give children who live in chaos a chance to learn to trust.

One way you can guide children toward managing their stress is to give them opportunities to shape their experiences while they are with you. Coping skills and strategies to reduce tension that are learned in the preschool and early elementary school years can last a lifetime.

There are many simple things children can do, such as stretching, tensing and relaxing muscles, and breathing exercises that will help them manage stress. Here are some examples:

Stretching: Have the children pretend to grow from a little, curled-up baby into a great, big giant.

Tensing and Relaxing Muscles: Have the children tense and relax their muscles like a machine that warms up all its parts, one at a time.

Breathing Exercises: Have the children breathe in warm, comforting air and imagine sending it to every part of the body.

Managing Fear

Fear is a natural part of childhood and can motivate children to develop healthy coping skills, which increases their personal security level.

Fears are very real for young children and include the subjective, intangible types and the possible but unlikely ones. Because some fears are less likely to occur, guiding children toward mastering them can be tricky. It requires imagination, symbolism, and creativity from adults.

The goal is to build perceptions of safety that will harness fears rather than forget them. It is easy for adults to not take children's fears seriously. Making fun of children's fears will only intensify their insecurities. Trying to talk them out of their fears rarely works. Children need help learning how to address their fears.

How you help them depends on their developmental stage. Preschool children may benefit from opportunities to confront fierce monsters or gigantic dragons through stories and symbolic play. Elementary-age children can begin to master their fears on a more direct and personal basis through art and literary activities.

Open-ended questions can prompt children to use their imaginations for rebuilding their perceptions of security:

I wonder what you might be able to do to feel safer and stronger? What might you use to help you do that?

If you could turn that monster into a friend, what kind of a friend would you choose it to be? How do you think you might make that happen?

Is the monster afraid of a certain kind of noise, music, or light? How can you make that work for you?

Pay close attention to guiding the children toward nonviolent solutions, without rejection or criticism.

Managing Conflict

The ability to successfully manage conflict is an essential building block for resiliency. Conflict resolution requires mutual acceptance and acknowledgment of the interests and needs of each person in the disagreement. Your setting can provide an environment and opportunity for building the communication skills necessary for managing stress. You can help children learn to diffuse intense feelings and identify the needs of each person involved. Resolution skills learned early can help these children lead happier, less stressful lives.

Children need to learn what successful conflict management requires:

Everyone involved in a conflict needs to define the problem as they see it.

Everyone involved in the conflict participates equally in building the solution.

Everyone is valued equally, despite any differences in title or power based on a role.

Everyone is committed to building a solution that has mutual benefits for all.

Everyone is opposed to anyone winning, blaming, or imposing punishments.

Conflict management is best taught by example. The most effective learning tool is the way the adults around children resolve their differences. When there are disparities of role power between adults and children, it is important for the adults to make the first move. They can better afford to take the risk to restore trust to a relationship.

Participating in Own Safety

Children are growing up in a violent society. For some their very survival may depend on their ability to manage their own safety. Your environment may be the only place in which these skills can be learned, and the children's intuition about their own safety can be affirmed.

Help children recognize and respect the physical clues their bodies give them to alert them to something unsafe. Those clues can include fast breathing, heavy heart beats, tummy rumblings, cold sweaty hands, a lump in the throat, or tingling sensations up the back and on the arms.

All children will have sensed some of these, perhaps while watching a video. The key is what young children do about these signals. If they have been told feeling fear is weak, they will learn to discount the clues and ignore the warnings. Children who have been urged to always obey their elders may suppress such clues and remain passive. These behaviors can increase their chances of becoming a victim of their personal fears or a dangerous situation.

You can empower children to believe in their ability to stay safe. Ask them what they can do to help keep themselves safe since adults may not always be available. Affirm that children have the right to say "No" whenever a situation is confusing or they do not feel comfortable.

Assist children in learning how, when, and where danger starts. Ask them questions to get them to think about their safety: What are your first body clues that something may be wrong? What can you do when you feel those clues? Can you run, make noise, or yell?

"What If..." games or exercises can be helpful to play: What if you were in a mall restroom and someone cornered you? What if a strange car pulled up close to you and asked for directions? What if a stranger asked you to help find a lost puppy?

Providing a Violence-Free Environment

An important requirement for all adults who are concerned with building resiliency in children is a personal commitment to nonviolence. Children can build hope for the future only when safety and hope are integrated into their life experiences and environments.

Sometimes caring adults can feel disheartened that their efforts and relationships with the children they care for are easily over-shadowed or discounted by the experiences the children have when they leave their environment. Be assured, you do have a strong and long-term influence on the children you care for and teach.

As their teacher or caregiver you have the opportunity to model and build with the children an environment free from fear and shame. You may be the only advocate for nonviolence they have known in their young lives.

Through your presence and teaching you have a unique opportunity to nurture the resiliency of children by your commitment to nonviolence and personal practice of the resiliency-building skills.

The children will benefit by the environment you establish. By example you can teach children many of these important skills:

To recognize conflict as normal. It is an opportunity to build a new sense of community and connectedness.

To honor all feelings and use the energy of anger and fear to work out problems fairly and safely.

To resist using competition and judgments to separate or reject others.

To trust personal intuition and use it to guide oneself and others toward nonviolence.

To resist using punishments to correct problems but to focus on others' strengths.

To listen for the needs of conflict with our partners and to work together to solve problems.

To use one's head and heart to build fair resolutions.

To teach that no one is safe unless everyone is safe.

Resources

Resolving Conflict Creatively Program
103 Third Avenue
New York, NY 10003
(212) 387-0225

Begun, Ruth Weltman. *Ready to Use Social Skills Lessons and Activities, Pre-K-12.* Center for Applied Research in Education: West Nyak, NY, 1995.

Center to Prevent Handgun Violence. *STAR Curriculum: Straight Talk About Risks.* Washington, DC: Center to Prevent Handgun Violence, 1992.

Drew, Naomi. *Learning the Skills of Peacemaking: An Activity Guide for Elementary-Age Children on Communicating, Cooperating and Resolving Conflict.* Rolling Hills Estates, CA: Jalmar Press, 1995.

Embry, Dennis. *Peacebuilders.* Tucson, AZ: Heartsprings, 1993.

Henderson, Nan and Mike M. Milstein. *Resiliency in Schools: Making it Happen for Students and Educators.* Thousands Oaks, CA: Corwin Press, Inc., 1996.

Kaufman, Gershen and Lev Raphael. *Stick Up For Yourself.* Minneapolis: Free Spirit, 1990.

Mendler, Allen N. *Smiling at Yourself—Educating Young Children About Stress and Self-Esteem.* Santa Cruz, CA: Network Publications, 1990.

Schmidt, Fran and Alice Friedman. *Peacemaking Skills for Little Kids.* Miami Beach, FL: Grace Contrino Abrams Peace Education, 1993.

Shure, Myrna B. *I Can Problem Solve: An Interpersonal/Cognitive Problem-Solving Program.* Champaign, IL: Research Press, 1992.

Slaby, Ronald G., Wendy C. Roedell, Diana Arezzo, and Kate Hendrix. *Early Violence Prevention: Tools for Teachers of Young Children.* Washington, DC: National Association for the Education of Young Children, 1995.

Children's Books

Barrett, Joyce Durham. *Willie's Not the Hugging Kind.* New York: Harper Collins Children's Books, 1989.

Blackburn, Lynn. *I Know I Made It Happen.* Omaha, NE: Centering Corporation, 1991.

Crary, Elizabeth. *I'm Frustrated.* Seattle: Parenting Press, 1992.

———. *I'm Mad.* Seattle: Parenting Press, 1992.

Hazen, Barbara. *Even If I Did Something Awful.* New York: Aladdin Books, 1992.

Klamath County YMCA Family Preschool. *The Land of Many Colors.* New York: Scholastic Inc., 1993.

Shapiro, Lawrence. *The Very Angry Day That Amy Didn't Have.* King of Prussia, PA: Child's Work/Child's Play, 1994.

Williams, Arlene. *Tales From The Dragon's Cave: Peace-Making Stories for Everyone.* Sparks, NV: The Waking Light Press, 1995.

Appendix

Making Referrals

The symbolic healing activities offered in this book are not intended to be a substitute for the range of community mental health services available to children through many public and private systems. Neither are they to be used as a substitute for reporting suspected child abuse to the appropriate local authorities. All educators and caregivers are mandated to report suspected child abuse.

This book is offered as a practical guide for adults who want to provide children with active ways to integrate their life experiences with their experiences in schools, centers, or any other group settings. The activities are designed to help empower children and give them hope for their future.

The healing activities presented in this book can be used as reinforcement for children who might be receiving community mental health services. It is possible that the introduction of a healing exercise may alert you to a child who appears to need referral to professional mental health services.

The decision by a teacher or caregiver to make a referral is usually the culmination of a caring, introspective evaluation. To refer a child for mental health services is as much a part of any comprehensive educational program as arranging for a math or reading tutor. It is the sign of an insightful adult who respects and cares for children.

How to Tell if a Child Needs to Be Referred

The child is so depressed or withdrawn, regular classroom, program, or playground participation is no longer possible.

The child has become highly aggressive, or outbursts are so intense, that the safety of the child or others is at risk.

The child has spoken or written of suicidal behavior or other intentions to harm him or herself.

The child reports to have heard voices or seen things others are unable to validate.

What You Can Do to Help

Develop a trusting relationship with a child's parent(s) or guardians to learn what their insights are into possible reasons for the child's behaviors and experiences. These might include household moves, fires, the loss of a pet, the loss of an important adult relationship, a new sibling, a change in the health of a family member, or economic changes.

Become familiar with the local agencies that provide services for children and their families.

Keep a behavioral log that records the specific dates and types of troubling behavior. This could strengthen your recommendation for referral and provide significant information for the eventual service provider.

Inform parents of your observations and concerns, even in cases of suspected child abuse.

Inquire if the child is now or ever has received counseling and if the parents have any preferred agencies.

Honor the confidentiality of the child and family when securing services for a child.

Allow parent(s) to initiate services with the agency of their choice.

Allow the parent(s) to set the date for the next appointment with you as a continuation of your support for them.

Your success in encouraging the parent(s) to carry through on the referral is crucial to the process. Offer to walk the parents through the process. Explain what it will mean for them. Tell them how you can help and support them. Your relationship with the parent(s) will be a vital part of securing the needed services for the child.

Your commitment to the child's long-term well-being may be your best ally in working with the parent(s). It will also be your finest professional characteristic.

If you sense it would be welcomed, form a team with another staff member who also has a trusting relationship with the child and parent(s), to reinforce your efforts to support the family.

Making referrals can be frightening for adults. Others may discourage you by saying you are over-reacting. It is essential that you follow your thoughtful observation and strong intuitions, based on a relationship with the child, to follow through in every way necessary to get the help the child needs. You may be the person who literally saves the child's life, physically or psychologically. Empower yourself and do what you believe is best for the children.

Additional Resources

Barlin, Anne Lief and Nurit Kalev. *Goodnight Toes! Bedtime Stories, Lullabies, and Movement Games.* Pennington, NJ: Princeton Book Company, 1993.

——. *Hello Toes? Movement Games for Children.* Pennington, NJ: Princeton Book Company, 1991.

Beland, Kathleen R. *Second Step.* Seattle: Committee For Children, 1987.

Benzwie, Teresa. *A Moving Experience: Dance for Lovers of Children and the Child Within.* Tucson, AZ: Zephyr Press, 1987.

——. *More Moving Experiences: Connecting Arts, Feelings, and Imagination.* Tucson, AZ: Zephyr Press, 1995.

Bureau of At-Risk Youth. *The Strong Kids Program: A Life Skills Program that Helps Build Intellectually, Socially and Emotionally Strong Kids.* Huntington, NY: Bureau of At-Risk Youth, 1991.

Cooper, Sally J. *New Strategies For Free Children: Child Abuse Prevention for Elementary School Children.* Lima, OH: National Child Abuse Prevention Center, 1991.

Curwin, Richard L. and Allen Mendler. *Am I In Trouble? Using Discipline To Teach Young Children Responsibility.* Santa Cruz, CA: ETR Associates, 1990.

Fugitt, Eva, D. *He Hit Me Back First: Self-Esteem Through Self-Discipline.* Rolling Hills Estates, CA: Jalmar Press, 1983.

Gabarino, James. *Let's Talk About Living In A World of Violence.* Chicago: The Erikson Institute, 1993.

Gliko-Braden, Majel. *Grief Comes To Class.* Omaha: Centering Corporation, 1992.

Grotberg, Edith. *A Guide to Promoting Resilience in Children.* The Hague, The Netherlands: Bernard van Leer Foundation, 1995.

Higgins, Gina O'Connell. *Resilient Adults: Overcoming a Cruel Past.* San Francisco: Jossey Bass Publishers, 1995.

Kaufman, Bobbie and Agnes Wohl. *Casualties of Childhood: A Developmental Perspective on Sexual Abuse Using Projective Drawings.* New York: Brunner-Mazel, Inc., 1992.

Kent, Lisa. *Someone Cries For the Children.* Rolling Hills Estates, CA: Jalmar Press, 1994.

Klepsch, Marvin and Laura Logie. *Children Draw and Tell: An Introduction to the Projective Uses of Children's Human Figure Drawings.* New York: Brunner-Mazel, 1982.

Kohn, Alfie. *Punished By Rewards: The Trouble With Gold Stars...and Other Bribes.* New York: Houghton Mifflin Co., 1993.

Levin, Diane, E. *Teaching Young Children In Violent Times.* Cambridge, MA: Educators for Social Responsibility, 1994.

Magid, K., and C. McKelvey. *High Risk: Children Without a Conscience.* New York: Bantam Books, 1987.

Malchiodi, Cathy. *Breaking the Silence: Art Therapy with Children from Violent Homes.* New York: Brunner-Mazel, 1990.

McCracken, Janet Brown. *Reducing Stress in Young Children's Lives.* Washington, DC: National Association for the Education of Young Children, 1986.

McGillis, E., and A. Goldstein. *Skillstreaming the Elementary School Child: A Guide to Teaching Presocial Skills.* Champaign, IL: Research Press Co., 1984.

Metcalf, Linda. *Counseling Toward Solutions: A Practical Solution-Focused Program for Working with Students, Teachers and Parents.* West Nyack, NY: The Center for Applied Research in Education, 1995.

Morrow, Gertrude. *The Compassionate School.* Englewood Cliffs, NJ: Prentice-Hall, Inc., 1987.

Osofsky, Joy D. *Children, Youth and Violence: Searching for Solutions.* New York: The Guilford Press, 1995.

Peled, Einat and Diane Davis. *Groupwork With Children of Battered Women.* Thousand Oaks, CA: Sage Publications, 1995.

Reynolds, Rebecca A. *Bring Me the Ocean: Nature as Healer, Messenger and Intermediary.* Action, MA: Vander & Burham, 1995.

Rubin, Judith. *Child Art Therapy.* New York: Van Nostrand Reinhold Co., 1984.

Schaefer, C. and K. O'Connor, eds. *Handbook of Play Therapy.* New York: John Wiley & Sons, 1983.

Smith, Charles A. *The Peaceful Classroom. 162 Easy Activities To Teach Preschoolers Compassion & Cooperation.* Beltsville, MD: Gryphon House, 1993.

Strauss, Murray A. *Beating the Devil Out of Them: Corporal Punishment in American Families.* New York: Lexington Books, 1994.

Sullivan, Molly. *Movement: Exploration for Young Children.* Washington, DC: National Association for the Education of Young Children, 1982.

Terr, Lenore. "Childhood Traumas: An Outline and Review." *American Journal of Psychiatry* 148, (1991): 10-20.

Vernon, Ann. *Thinking, Feeling, Behaving: An Emotional Education Curriculum for Children and Adolescents.* Champaign, IL: Research Press Co., 1989.

Wohl, Agnes and Bobbie Kaufman. *Silent Screams and Hidden Cries: An Interpretation of Artwork by Children from Violent Homes.* New York: Brunner-Mazel, Inc., 1985.

Children's Books

Blackburn, Lynn. *The Class in Room 414.* Omaha: Centering Corporation, 1987.

Campbell, James A. *The Secret Places.* Omaha: Centering Corporation, 1992.

Conlin, Susan and Susan Levine Friedman. *All My Feelings At Home: Ellie's Day.* Seattle: Parenting Press, 1989.

Edwards, Elsy. *Sandy's Suitcase.* New York: SRA, Macmillan/McGraw Hill, 1994.

Ferguson, Dorothy. *A Bunch of Balloons.* Omaha: Centering Corporation, 1990.

Gifaldi, David. *The Boy Who Spoke Colors.* Boston: Houghton Mifflin Co., 1993.

Kaiser Johnson, Lee and Sue Kaiser Johnson. *If I Ran the Family.* Minneapolis: Free Spirit Publishing, 1992.

Janover, Caroline. *Josh: A Boy With Dyslexia.* Burlington, VT: Waterfront Books, 1988.

Lamb, Nancy. *One April Morning.* New York: Lothrop, Lee & Shepard, 1996.

Marcus, Irene and Paul Marcus. *Scary Night Visitors.* New York: Magination Press, 1990.

Masoer, Adolph. *Don't Feed The Monster on Tuesday: A Children's Self-Esteem Book.* Kansas City, MO: Landmark Editions, Inc., 1988.

Morrissey, Dean. *Ship of Dreams*. Kirkland, WA: Abrams, 1994.

Olofsdotter, Marie. *Sofia and the Heartmenders*. Minneapolis: Free Spirit Publishing, 1993.

Powell, Richard. *How to Deal With Monsters*. Mahwah, NJ: Watermill Press, 1990.

Ross, Christine. *Lily and the Bears*. New York: Houghton Mifflin Co., 1991.

Ross, Tony. *Happy Blanket*. New York: Farrar, Strauss & Giroux, 1990.

Shapiro, Lawrence. *The Very Angry Day That Amy Didn't Have*. King of Prussia, PA: Child's Work/Child's Play, 1994.

Shles, Larry. *Aliens In My Nest*. Rolling Hills Estates, CA: Jalmar Press, 1982.

———. *Hoots & Toots & Hairy Brutes*. Rolling Hills Estates, CA: Jalmar Press, 1989.

———. *Hugs & Shrugs*. Rolling Hills Estates, CA: Jalmar Press, 1987.

Steig, William. *Spinky Sulks*. Singapore: Sunburst Books, 1988.

Stein, Sara Bonnett. *On Divorce: An Open Family Book*. New York: Walker and Company, 1984.

Varley, Susan. *Badger's Parting Gifts*. New York: Morrow, 1984.

Vigna, Judith. *Grandma Without Me*. Niles, IL: Albert Whitman, 1984.

———. *She's Not My Real Mother*. Niles, IL: Albert Whitman, 1980.

Viorst, Judith. *Alexander and The Terrible Horrible No Good Very Bad Day*. New York: Aladdin Books, 1972.

Williams, Arlene. *Tales From The Dragon's Cave: Peacemaking Stories for Everyone*. The Sparks, NV: Waking Light Press, 1995.

Willis, Jeanne and Susan Varley. *The Monster Bed*. Lothrop, Lee & Shepard, 1986.

White, E.B. *Charlotte's Web*. New York: Harper & Row, 1952.

About the Author

Barbara Oehlberg completed a graduate program in child development at the University of Akron in 1981 after receiving a degree in home economics from the University of Wisconsin and raising seven children.

Recognizing that children learn violence primarily within their families, she combined her peace activism with her profession and created a program for the Ohio Governor's Office (Celeste) in 1983 entitled "Parenting for Peaceful Families." She has facilitated that program in Ohio's schools, churches, and prisons.

As a family life specialist with the Cleveland Public Schools, Barbara has seen firsthand how domestic violence, child abuse, and stress can affect children's behaviors and learning abilities.

Index: Activity Titles

Index: Activities by Issues

Other Redleaf Press Publications

All the Colors We Are: The Story of How We Get Our Skin Color — Outstanding full-color photographs showcase the beautiful diversity of human skin color, and offers children a simple, accurate explanation.

The Kindness Curriculum: Introducing Young Children To Loving Values — Over 60 imaginative, exuberant activities that create opportunities for kids to practice kindness, empathy, conflict resolution, respect, etc.

Practical Solutions to Practically Every Problem: The Early Childhood Teacher's Manual — Over 300 proven developmentally appropriate solutions for all kinds of classroom problems.

Roots & Wings: Affirming Culture in Early Childhood Programs — A new approach to multicultural education that helps shape positive attitudes toward cultural differences.

Those Mean Nasty Dirty Downright Disgusting but...Invisible Germs — A delightful story that reinforces for children the benefits of frequent hand washing.

Training Teachers: A Harvest of Theory and Practice — Original strategies and training tools that bring a new approach to the how of teaching that supports great teacher development.

Transition Magician: Strategies for Guiding Young Children in Early Childhood Programs — Over 200 original, fun activities that help you magically turn transition times into calm, smooth activity changes.

For the Love of Children: Daily Affirmations For People Who Care for Children — An empowering book, yet warm and gentle. For those people who spend most of their waking hours caring for and about children.

Prime Times: A Handbook for Excellence in Infant and Toddler Programs — Guides you through the organization of a program of excellent care and education for infants and toddlers. Assists you in staffing the program with those who will maintain the vital quality of caregiving you establish.

Open the Door Let's Explore More! Field Trips of Discovery for Young Children — Filled with activities to do before, during and after delightful field trips. Reinforce learning while having fun.

Reflecting Children's Lives: A Handbook for Planning Child-Centered Curriculum — Shows how to put children's needs at the center of your curriculum while dealing with all aspects of young children's programs.

So This is Normal Too? Teachers and Parents Working Out Developmental Issues in Young Children — Makes the challenging behaviors of children a vehicle for cooperation among adults and stepping stones to learning for children.

Call Redleaf Press toll free
to order or for a catalog
1-800-423-8309